When Grief Visits School

Second Edition

Organizing a Successful Response

by

Dr. John Dudley

A Resource for Administrators, Counselors, and Other Staff

Copyright 1995, 2003 John Dudley

ISBN 1-930572-23-9

Library of Congress Control Number 2003108040

Printing (Last Digit)

9   8   7   6   5   4   3   2   1

Publisher—
Educational Media Corporation®
P.O. Box 21311
Minneapolis, MN 55421-0311
(763) 781-0088 or (800) 966-3382
www.**educationalmedia**.com

Production Editor—
Don L. Sorenson

Graphic Design—
Earl R. Sorenson

About the Author

John Dudley has trained over 5,000 school crisis response teams across America and has helped schools deal with the deaths of more than 2,600 students and staff. At the request of the Oklahoma City school district, Dr. Dudley led the response in their schools after the bombing of the federal building. John has helped numerous communities respond to violent tragedies, including communities directly impacted by the events of September 11, 2001. He is the former Supervisor of Counseling Services for the Lincoln, Nebraska schools and is president of Crisis Management, LLC. His website is www.schoolcrisis.org.

Dedication

The second edition of this book is dedicated to the thousands of school crisis team members across America I have had the opportunity to meet. Your efforts to help students and staff in schools affected by tragedies have positively impacted countless lives. My work with you, difficult at times as it has been, has had a positive impact on my life. Thank you for all you have done and continue to do.

Preface

The first edition of *When Grief Visits School: Organizing a Successful Response* has been read by thousands of people. As the author of this book, I have had the unusual experience of talking to many people who have read it and used it as a teaching tool in hundreds of school crisis training workshops. The book has been well received, and I am pleased it has been of direct help to many schools in responding to tragedies.

One of the most unusual responses to the first edition was via a phone call. Early one morning I answered the phone in my office only to hear a voice on the other end of the line say, "I am on page 89 of your book and I am reading as fast as I can! About an hour ago a student in our school was killed. I grabbed your book off of my bookshelf and am using it to guide me as I prepare to lead my school's crisis team. Are there any parts of the book to which I need to pay particular attention?"

I would like to think the entire first edition was worth "particular attention." I hope this second edition only enhances the first. In this second edition I have tried to maintain the integrity of the first book as well as to add some "After Thoughts" based on my experiences and what I have learned since. Additionally, I have added information on preventing violence in schools, and if a school's efforts in preventing violence were not successful, some thoughts on responding to violent events in schools. Over the years it has been my privilege to train and learn from hundreds of law enforcement officers at the local, state, and federal level. This edition shares with you some of the things they taught me.

Ever since I began training school staffs to successfully respond to tragedies, I have always said I hoped they would not have to use anything they learned from me. The second edition of this book was written in my further quest to share what I have experienced and learned in helping schools manage crisis events. It is my hope you will never have to use anything you might learn from reading this book. God forbid, if you ever have to grab it off of your bookshelf and rapidly read to "page 89" and beyond, it is my wish that you will find it of assistance.

Table of Contents

An Overview

The phone rings in the middle of the night and jars me from sleep. Is this just another crank call for my teenage daughter? "Hello, hello," I more or less shout at the phone receiver. A voice at the other end has a faint familiarity. By now, my brain is beginning to function at almost a normal level. It's Mary Warren, the principal at River City Elementary School. She is upset and asking for help. She launches into an explanation of her concerns. I turn on the light and look for something to take notes.

I hear sobbing. "They're all dead! The entire family. Dead!!"

By now I am more than awake. Scrap paper for notes and an old dull pencil have suddenly appeared at the top of the junk pile in the drawer. "Mary, talk to me. Tell me what is going on. Mary, are you all right?"

"It's the Carmichael's. They are all dead. Little Sarah, Tom, his wife, Bill, the one we had in elementary school, and Brad. He was in his first year of college. Dead!"

Everything is running at full speed now. I am trying to hold the scrap of paper still and write down names.

"Sarah, was she a student in your school? What grade?"

"She was a fifth grader. She's dead. I just saw her Friday. She was in Mrs. Kerry's room. She had the prettiest blond hair down to her shoulders. We have had her since kindergarten. Bright, and could she sing. She sang a solo at the holiday performance. Could she sing. I wish you could have heard her."

"Mary, tell me what happened. What do you know?"

"I got a call from Bill Larsen. I had him as a student way back when. You know, Lt. Larsen, with the police. He said he thought I ought to know before I heard it on the morning news. He said they got a call from a neighbor who heard strange noises on Saturday. Why they waited until Sunday night to call the police I don't know. Mrs. Carmichael was PTA president two years ago. She was always willing to help out when we needed her."

"Mary, what else did Lt. Larsen tell you?"

"They always seemed like such a nice family, the Carmichael's. He said they were investigating it as a quadruple murder and suicide. Something about a letter they found. They think Mr. Carmichael wrote it.

I don't know how I am ever going to be able to tell my staff. Don't you think we should have a staff meeting before school? We are an early start school, you know. I don't have a policy book at home. Aren't we supposed to have a calling tree or something like that? I always said I would make a copy of that policy and have it here at home. Guess I say that about a lot of things, but you know how busy things get."

"What information did Bill Larsen give you?"

"He said they found the whole family about 10:15 last night—mother, father, Sarah, and her two brothers. They had all been shot. Did I tell you I saw Sarah at school on Friday?"

"Did the police give you any other information?"

"They think it was murder, suicide. There was a letter. Guess I told you that. I'm sorry I woke you up so early. I remembered you saying one time in a meeting something about getting as much information as early as possible. I know it's early. I guess they are predicting a little snow. That's all we need!!"

"Mary, have you called anyone else?"

"Heavens, no! Not at this hour."

"Can you think of anything else I need to know before we plan how we are going to work with your staff and students?"

"I hope you have one of those policy books at home. Mine's at school."

"Mary, do you have a copy of your calling tree at home?"

"It's with my policy book."

"How about your assistant principal? Would he have one?"

"You know, I need to call Dean and tell him what happened. He will be devastated. If I remember, he had Brad, Sarah's older brother, in his room. I don't know how I'll tell him. He will be so upset."

"Mary, let me call Dean. I'll see if he has the calling tree list and tell him we will get back to him in a few minutes. If he doesn't have the list, who else might have it?"

"Would you call him? Oh, thanks! I need to get dressed and try to figure out how I am going to handle this."

"Can you think of anyone else who has the list at home?"

"Our media specialist may have it. She is a detail person. She has bailed me out before on things like this. I always feel like I owe her."

"Call her. I'll call Dean. Let's plan to be on the phone for only a couple of minutes. It is 5:20 now. I'll call you back at 5:30. Then we will know if you have to go to school to get the list. It's a list of both certified and classified staff, isn't it?"

"I think so. I told my secretary to make it up that way. I think so."

"I will call you in ten minutes. Remember, it is very important that you don't tie up your phone. I'll talk to you in a few minutes."

Dean's line was busy. Mary decided to call Dean because she did not want him to hear the news from someone else.

I called the school district's crisis response team leader and gave the basic details. According to procedure, the leader is to notify team members and schedule an early morning meeting.

The Crisis Response Team

Crisis response teams are established to assist in managing tragedies that have significant impact on schools, i.e., student or staff deaths, critically ill or injured students/staff, terminal illness, natural disasters, hostage or abduction situations. These teams are designed to provide assistance to students and staff, preschool through high school.

The selection criteria for members of crisis response teams focus on certified and classified staff who have an interest in crisis response, are willing to receive training, have the respect of fellow staff, and can maintain a "non-anxious presence" in times of considerable stress. All team members should be capable of successfully working with students pre-K through 12

It's 5:30 and Mary's phone is busy. I call the school district's contact at the police department. Information is still sketchy. I learn the police suspect the mother, daughter, and high school son were probably murdered sometime Friday night. It appears, according to the letter left at the scene, that the husband killed them. I also learn the husband traveled to the college campus of the oldest son and brought him back home on Saturday. My "source" thinks he may have been murdered Saturday night and the husband killed himself on Sunday. The police will have more information available by mid-morning and promise to share it with me before they hold a press conference.

At 5:40 Mary's line is still busy. I touch base with the team leader and agree to have a crisis response team meeting at 6:30.

I called the school superintendent and was greeted with, "Something really bad must have happened for you to call at this hour." We talked about the situation and I asked the superintendent to notify the high school principal. I agreed to call the high school principal around 6:00 a.m. to share more information and discuss a plan for the day.

The General Plan

As the old saying goes, "People don't plan to fail, they fail to plan." Ellen Flax stated in her *Education Week* article Flax, Ellen. "Aftermath: 'I would panic but I would stick to my plan' ", Education Week, Vol. 8, Issue 18, Page 5, January 25, 1989. "Last week's school yard killing spree in Stockton, California dramatically demonstrated the need for school officials to develop a plan for (crisis response)...." During an emergency, said Lynda Lewis, principal of Stanton College Preparatory School in Jacksonville, Florida, who has helped develop emergency plans for Duval County schools since 1981, "I would be upset, I would panic, but I would follow my plan" (Flax, 1989).

The general plan for crisis response is an outline of the steps school personnel should take during a tragedy. The plan is an over-view of the process at school to assist students, staff, and parents during a crisis.

The ring of my phone startled me. It was Mary.

"I have been trying to get a hold of you for the last fifteen minutes!! Dean had the phone tree list and he is calling staff."

"Did you tell him to tell the teachers to come to school early?" I inquire, trying to hide my concern that the cart is getting ahead of the horse. "Our district crisis plan suggests that we have a staff meeting before school."

"I should have a copy of that plan here at home. I never, in my wildest dreams, thought anything like this would ever happen. I told Dean to tell them what happened. That's all...."

"The crisis response team plans to meet at 6:30 this morning. If we can get a copy of your calling tree list, we can have some of the team members call staff and tell them to come to school early for a meeting. Don't worry, it won't be a big problem," I halfheartedly tried to convince the both of us. "Let's meet at your school at 7:00 a.m. to talk about how we can help you. I will have a team of six people at the meeting."

"What if I start crying? You know they put glass windows along the front of my office. And those drapes I ordered never did fit right. They're in a box in my closet. What will I do if I lose it in front of everyone?"

"Let's talk about that when we get together at seven. I'll be there by then, or a little before. Remember, we have a lot of experience in handling these kinds of things. We will be able to help you to help your students and staff. See you at seven."

I hang up muttering to myself, "What do I mean WE have a lot of experience in handling these kinds of things? Single deaths, yes, but this is a first."

As I try to break the record for getting dressed, the phone rings. It is a local radio station. My blood pressure rises. "No, I do not have many details. Yes, I will be working with the elementary school and the high school." The high school!!! I quickly excuse myself and call the high school principal.

The Media

A school's response to a crisis should not only be appropriate, it should look good. Today's headlines frequently scream aloud what is wrong, but seldom announce what is right. America's schools seem to be the focus of blame on many issues. Educators are proficient in managing schools but, by and large, they are not trained in working with the media. During times of crisis, working successfully with all facets of the media frequently depends on a foundation of cooperation and understanding built prior to the event at hand as well as school staff who have the skill and knowledge of successfully working with the media.

After a brief discussion, I agree with the high school principal to send two district crisis team members to help there. The high school counselors in the school will be recruited to help, even though the crisis plan suggests that they be available to work with students who may not be directly affected by the events of the day. I give myself a brief lecture for not setting up two crisis teams and make a feeble promise to do that when this is over.

A glass of juice serves as breakfast—not knowing that it will be my only "meal" that day —while I jot down some notes. Why didn't we get more organized? I chide myself for putting things off.

At the 6:30 crisis team meeting I go over the details of the tragedy as best I can. One of the team members is ill. I had thoughts about setting up a procedure for using substitutes on the team but never got it organized. My promise to send two team members to the high school may not be possible until later in the morning. They'll understand, I hope.

The crisis team has practiced many times. We have developed scenarios for the practice sessions: accidents, terminal illness, teacher or student death, suicide, natural disaster, but no scenario on quadruple murders.

The team, consisting of an elementary, middle level, and high school counselor; a school psychologist; and two family specialists (school social workers), is ready to go. The high school counselor, a member of the team, is ill. He's one of the two people I was going to send to the high school. They'll understand, I reassure myself again.

The team leader brought coffee and rolls. Why didn't I think of that, I ask myself and then remember that the morning has been busy, to say the least.

After sharing all of the information I have, the team begins to design a specific plan. Issues to be considered include: an early morning staff meeting, help in some of the classrooms, working with the media, contacting concerned parents, a crisis room for students and staff (two different rooms), keeping the school open in the evening for parents, an end of the day staff meeting, splitting the team between two schools, getting subs for teachers who may not be able to teach, contacting other schools in the district and helping them with concerns, handling the possessions of the dead students, writing a letter to be sent to all of the parents of both the elementary and high school, and enclosing some materials that may be helpful in assisting their students at home. We will share our plan with the building principal and get her input.

The Specific Plan

There is a significant difference between a general plan to manage school tragedy and a specific plan to handle particular events. The specific plan, usually developed under the pressure of time, is a detailed set of procedures that can enable schools to be successful in minute by minute crisis management. This plan takes into account the nuances of crisis response and a strategy to manage the crisis at hand.

The team arrives at the elementary school at 6:55. The building is locked. We wait.

At 7:15 Mary arrives. Teachers have been calling her at home for more information and to share their feelings. Mary looks exhausted and on the verge of tears. The team silently follows her down the hall to her office.

After some brief introductions, the team leader outlines the plan. Mary listens and intermittently offers suggestions that are incorporated into the plan. We all share some concerns regarding how we think some students might respond to the situation. Two team members are assigned the task of drafting an announcement to students for Mary's final editing and approval.

The Announcement

How students and staff learn about the crisis frequently sets the tone for their response. One school, a few years ago, held an assembly to tell their students that two of their classmates had been killed in a car accident. Some students, who were especially close friends of those who were killed, became hysterical and more students were distraught than if the announcement had been made in classrooms. Further, the school should have first identified close friends of the students who were killed and told them either individually or in small groups.

The announcement of a tragedy needs to be carefully crafted and the method for making the announcement needs to be given considerable thought.

The staff begins to arrive. As the team completes the final preparations for the morning meeting, I walk the halls. Overall, the staff is subdued. Some appear afraid. I overhear such comments as, "This reminds me of the day after President Kennedy was shot." "I remember the day the space shuttle exploded...." "This brings back too many bad memories about my own family." "I'm glad that SOB killed himself or I would have done it for him!"

The three short rings of the bell indicate the staff meeting is about to begin. Staff enter the room in small groups. Some staff stand toward the back of the media center. They seem uneasy and not certain of what to expect. There are tears, somber faces, and few smiles.

Mary thanks the staff for coming early and reminds them that she had held a staff meeting earlier in the school year and shared the school crisis plan which called for an early morning staff meeting. Somewhat haltingly, but in a calm manner, she begins to relate the events as she knows them.

"My sister died and I miss her so much," a voice screams from the back of the room. Heads swivel. "We were twins. It wasn't my fault. If only I would have...." The custodian runs out of the room.

"As I was saying," Mary continues, "we will need to make a list of Sarah's friends. Barb," she looks to her right at a teacher sitting near the front of the room, "could you help with that?" The teacher nods affirmatively.

"Students will be arriving soon so I better introduce Nancy Stull. Nancy is here with some other people from the district to tell us what we can do to help students. When we had our staff meeting to discuss the function of the district crisis response team, none of us probably thought we'd ever need them. But now they are here to help us and we are glad to have them." Mary introduces the members of the crisis team and nods for Nancy to go ahead.

I watch as Nancy begins to outline the day. She discusses the options for making an announcement about Sarah and her family. Teachers are given the option of doing it themselves or having a crisis team member help them.

Substitutes will be available and can be used to give the teachers a short break or they will take classes for teachers who feel they can not remain at school. Teachers are encouraged to remain in school. In past crisis situations, students have been concerned something has happened to their teacher when the teacher has not been in the classroom.

Directions are given about where crisis team members will be located and how to access them. They will be assigned to places throughout the building—classrooms, office, halls, and the crisis center. Guidelines for sending students to the crisis center are explained.

The staff is reminded to use direct language—terms like dead, died, killed—not passed away, went to sleep, or God needed a good little girl in heaven.

Nancy talks about children and death. "Younger people often can't grasp the finality of death, but will need information about the details."

She cautions the teachers to expect a wide range of emotions from students. Among other things, the fear of losing a parent, relative, or dying themselves may develop. She points out that crisis events can trigger the surfacing of feelings around unresolved losses.

Several of the staff turn toward the back of the room to see if the janitor has returned. He has not.

Nancy encourages the staff to support one another through the days ahead. Staff is reminded that the team is there to help them as well as the students and parents.

Students are beginning to filter into the school. The meeting ends with information on memorials and a request for staff to avoid discussing the situation with anyone from the media and to direct all members of the media to the school office. Staff is requested to meet again after school.

Mary thanks Nancy and the team. A few clarifying questions are answered and the meeting is adjourned.

The Before School Staff Meeting

As the saying goes, "Timing is everything." If tragedy is going to visit your school, hope it doesn't come during the school day. The opportunity of having a staff meeting before school starts can be invaluable. Done properly, the before school meeting establishes a positive tone for the day(s) ahead. Considerable thought, planning, and skill are involved in the design of this meeting.

Sarah's teachers, who have been asked to remain for a brief meeting, gather in the front of the media center.

"How are you doing?" Nancy inquires informally.

"I don't handle things like this very well," blurts out one of the teachers.

"Most of us don't," reply several of the crisis team members.

"Would you like a couple of us to come to Sarah's home room and help you tell the kids?"

"That would be very helpful," responded the home room teacher.

"What if we cry?" two of them say almost simultaneously.

"Yes, what if I get started and can't stop. I cry when a bug hits my windshield," she says with a slight smile.

"No problem," comments one of the team. "Kids need to know that we are real people, too. Plus, it will send the signal to some of your students that it's OK for them to show emotions."

"Boys frequently have the biggest problem in these kinds of situations," another team member shares. "Don't be surprised if some of them get silly and act out. It's that old male macho stuff, you know."

The teachers reassure each other that they will make it through the morning. They dash down the hall and up the stairs hoping to beat most of the students to their rooms.

The Reaction of Students/Staff

No matter how competent school staffs are in effectively working with students, the stress and emotion of tragedy can affect the confidence and sometimes the skills of staff. Adults too often forget their own childhood needs and capabilities in handling crisis. Staff should be reminded of the developmental levels of students in handling the emotional impact of crisis events. These reminders help in assisting staff in dealing with student reactions. Parents can also benefit from hearing the same information.

I get to a phone and alert the high school about the ill crisis team member and lecture myself that, after this is all over, I will train some alternates to serve on the team. I share additional information with the high school principal and promise to arrive in his office not later than mid-morning. He assures me that not many of his students will be impacted by the tragedy and that his staff is very capable of handling the situation. Later I will regret not responding more quickly to the high school and my decision to only have one crisis response team to serve the entire school district.

The Problem of Under Responding

The "scramble" is not the dance of choice in crisis response. "Oops! This is a bigger deal than we thought it was going to be," are not the words of choice in crisis response.

Although it may be difficult initially to read the pulse of the event, making the mistake of under responding may create more problems. More often than not, it is easier to send crisis team members back to their "regular jobs" than to call them in a panic asking them to rush to a school. Although school personnel need to be prudent in all of their decisions, under responding to a tragedy may prove costly in both the short and long term.

Students laughing and running in the halls signals the beginning of another school week. This week will be a learning experience for children, adults, and an entire community. Little do I realize the depth of learning that will occur.

The first bell of the day calls the students to their classes. The strangers they see delivering announcements in their class-rooms will become friends and confidants before week's end. As one student said later, "They held me and rocked me just like my mom used to do before she went away. I didn't know Sarah very well, but it sure felt good to talk." Many of the stories coming out of the week will reinforce the fact that people, young or old, will share their deepest feelings and concerns with individuals they don't know. Given the fact that those individuals are well trained certainly helps.

The two crisis team members assigned to write the an-nouncement of Sarah's death, knowing that elementary children are in various stages of understanding regarding death, have written a simple straight forward announcement for the teach-ers to read to their students.

"Sarah Carmichael, a fifth grade student in our school, was killed this past weekend. Your teacher will share more informa-tion with you about Sarah's death. Please tell your teacher if you want to talk to someone about how you feel. Your teacher will talk with you or help you find someone with whom to talk."

Two crisis team members accompany Mrs. Keller, the fifth grade teacher who had Sarah in her classroom. They will help the teacher tell the students about Sarah's death. The plan is that after the teacher has shared the news with the 34 students in the fifth grade room, the students will be divided into three groups. It is hoped that students will do more sharing of feelings and concerns in the smaller groups.

Anticipation of another week of fun, and some learning, fills the halls as students visit with friends, put their belongings in lockers and drift into their classrooms. Most of the students entering Sarah's classroom ignore the visitors in their room and continue side conversations as they randomly pick their way to their desks. Today is Michele's birthday and she explains to her teacher that her mother is planning to come to school around 10:00 a.m. to bring treats for the class. Michele's teacher, trying to smile and greet the students, gently reminds Michele that school policy does not permit distributing treats. Tears of disappointment well up in Michele's eyes. Her teacher, nervously glancing at the classroom clock, assures Michele that it will be OK and that she will give Michele's mother a call and explain the no treat policy. Michele, head down, takes her seat.

"Children," the teacher said trying to quiet the students, "I hope you all had a good weekend," her voice beginning to tremble.

"I'm not a child!" exhorts a fifth grade boy.

"Students," correcting herself, "please quiet down and take your seats. I would like to introduce you to two helpers who have come to talk with us."

"These people," the teacher pointing to the two crisis team members, "have come to tell you some really bad news about Sarah. She was a wonderful girl and had so much potential, a great future. We are all going to miss her very much," concluded the teacher, now close to tears and thinking of escaping through the open classroom door.

The students, a little confused and exchanging nervous glances, turn toward the two members of the crisis team. The crisis team members move toward the front of the classroom, hoping that the teacher won't leave. One of the team members takes the teacher's hand while the other team member begins to address the students.

"Today your teacher is very sad because...." The process of telling the students about Sarah begins. The team helps them express their feelings and ideas related to Sarah's death and, for some students, the death of others, including pets.

Throughout the building the announcement of Sarah's death continued. As is often the case, reactions are varied. Some students come to the crisis room and are greeted by the elementary counselor and two members of the crisis team. The elementary counselor, who is eight months pregnant, has a temperature of 102 degrees and is planning to go home in about an hour.

Although the teachers at the staff meeting were asked to limit the number of students sent to the crisis center (the suggestion being no more than three students at any one time dismissed from their rooms to come to the crisis center), groups of six to eight students begin to arrive in the center. The crisis team leader, making the rounds checking on the team members and seeing how everything is progressing, helps out with the large number of students in the center.

The Crisis Center

Students and staff need a place to go when the events of the tragedy seem overwhelming. Sometimes people are not affected by the crisis at hand, but the crisis may trigger previous experiences that need addressing. The crisis room/center (there should be one for students and a separate one for staff, not the staff lounge) is usually staffed by members of the crisis team. If necessary, and if possible, a school counselor, teacher, or administrator may also assist at times.

After the students in Sarah's room have finished discussing Sarah's death in groups, they will talk about Sarah's classroom possessions and decide what to do with them. This is an activity that the crisis team has used before and found to be very successful with elementary students. They have discovered this helps many students deal with the finality of death and, put simply, to understand that Sarah is not coming back to school. This can be a difficult realization for some students, and the process of deciding what to do with Sarah's classroom possessions may help them. The crisis team also knows Sarah's teacher will probably feel better after this task. All too often, teachers alone clean out desks, lockers, and take down art work of deceased students as if they were never part of the school. This may meet the teacher's needs, but it usually is not helpful for the students in the room.

Dialogue among students in Sarah's classroom:

"Those books belong to the media center. I told Sarah she needed to return them, but you know her, she loved to read and wouldn't take books back until she finished them."

"Can I have her last art project? I want to take it home and hang it on the wall of my room."

"Look at the mess in this desk! Her room at home is the same way. Her mom was always yelling at her to clean it up. Guess her mom can't yell at her anymore. Just think, if I died, my mom couldn't yell at me."

"I don't want to help. I never liked her anyway."

"I don't want to help because I don't want to cry again."

"Can I have her locker? Then I won't have to share one."

"I am going to write a poem and put it in the burying box."

"It's called a basket or tasket or something like that, stupid."

"Casket," responds the teacher who, minute by minute, is gaining emotional strength.

Although one of the crisis team members has left Sarah's room, the other stays to assist the teacher and students. The plan is to have recess after the students have finished dealing with Sarah's possessions. The crisis team member reminds the teacher that, no matter what the normal time for recess, today the students need to go to recess right after this activity.

The Possessions of the Students

The proper disposition of the student's belongings can enhance the quality and effectiveness of the crisis team response. It can also assist students' understanding of the finality of death. Although one's tendency may be to quietly dispose of the dead student or staff member's possessions, the opportunity presents itself for another teachable moment. Don't miss it!

As the morning progresses, a sense of routine begins to flow back into the lives of many of the students. Although the ill elementary counselor has gone home, crisis team members continue their work with students and staff. Overhead projectors begin to light up, reading groups form, and the school moves toward the scheduled recess.

"Wouldn't you know it. I forgot my coat and it's colder than a well digger's you know what in the Klondike," comments one of the crisis team members. Three members of the team strategically place themselves on the playground so that they can interact with students and staff during recess. Students cluster in small groups, play games, run, and yell. A causal observer might conclude that nothing was out of the ordinary.

Crisis team members effectively work their way to each of the student groups. Conversation focuses on Sarah and her family. Guilt and anger pervade the conversations. Many students express remorse over not being able to tell Sarah good-bye or, for some, their recent actions toward Sarah. A few students openly discuss their wishes to go visit her, wherever she is, to tell her they are sorry for some of the things they did to her.

Crisis team members help where they can and enlist the aid of teachers in identifying the names of students for whom they have concerns. Too early for some and too late for others, the bell summons students to return to their classes.

The crisis team meets for a few minutes after recess break to assess the situation and check on each other. It appears, from a review of their notes, that eighty-four students thus far have had significant reactions to Sarah's death. Seventeen parents have been contacted and six students have gone home with their parents. The team would like to have four other students go home, but all four have working parents and the parents, when contacted by the team, would not make a commitment to leave work and remain home with their children.

Eight teachers have visited with team members about themselves or their concerns for other staff members. The team leader and one team member will follow-up during lunch with staff who have indicated they need help. The team leader will visit with staff who are concerned about others and make a determination as to how to proceed. One teacher has left the building and no one knows where he is. Repeated calls to his home have gone unanswered. It has been reported to the crisis team that the teacher has been very depressed for the past two months and has refused to seek professional help. One of the two subs, who were called in just in case any staff needed help or left the building, is covering the teacher's room. The other sub is rotating with several classrooms giving staff needed breaks.

The Management of Follow-Up

Throughout the course of a tragic event, attention to every detail is crucial. Nowhere is that more evident than follow-up. Every piece of information: every student, staff, and parent contact; every rumor; and every reaction needs to have an organized and efficient follow-up. Even when nothing is done about certain issues, the decision to do nothing should be a conscious decision. The quality of the response and its short and long term impact on those who need help makes well managed follow-up essential.

The morning progresses with minor adjustments in the crisis plan and, from the aroma in the halls, pizza is on the menu for lunch. Crisis team members were not included in the lunch count and will not be able to eat in the school cafeteria. "Each piece has about 10,000 calories." "I haven't eaten since I found out about this at 5:40 a.m." "I thought at our last crisis team practice session that we decided to have sack lunches brought in for team members." The team leader concludes the conversation among team members commenting, "I was on my way to order our lunches when I got recruited to help in here (the crisis center) and I forgot about it."

All students have left the student crisis room. Team members sort through the names of students determined to need follow-up before afternoon dismissal. Phone slips with the names of parents who have called the school and want to talk to "someone who is working on Sarah's murder" (there are forty-six phone slips) are distributed among crisis team members with the directions to call the parents when team members have time. Many of the calls will be made in the evening.

The principal stops by the crisis room. Her secretary has just completed typing the letter that will go home with all students at the end of the day. She wonders if the team members can help stuff envelopes and stick computerized address stickers on them. After a brief discussion, it is decided that two para-educators who work in the media center will help the secretary get the mailing ready to go home.

Mary notes that the secretary thinks the letter should not say that Sarah was killed. She thinks that statement is too direct and has changed the letter to read that Sarah has "passed away." The principal is ambivalent and wants the crisis team's opinion. The team leader reminds Mary of the early morning meeting when Mary was presented with a draft of a letter written by two crisis team members who have been trained to write this type of letter. She now remembers the rationale for using the term "killed," draws a line through passed away and inserts killed. The crisis team leader tells Mary that she wants to read the final draft of the letter after the secretary has completed typing it. The team leader remembers a previous situation when the letter was changed by a well intended staff member and does not want that problem to recur. The leader asks the principal if she is still planning to meet around 2:00 to plan the after school staff meeting. Mary acknowledges that the meeting is still on and excuses herself to finish her cafeteria duty.

The Letter

No single product of a good crisis response may be more important than the letter. This letter is sent to parents describing what has happened, what the school is doing about it, and it offers general suggestions for parents to help their children deal with the situation. It also conveys information about the funeral. This letter is the one consistent piece of communication provided to all parents. The letter reassures parents that everything is under control at school. It helps quell rumors and separates fact from fiction. Written well and used properly, it is one of the most powerful ingredients in the crisis response recipe.

Team members, sans lunch, return to their duties. They monitor classrooms and meet with students individually and in small groups. One team member devotes most of her time to working with staff and reminds herself that she should not be surprised at the number of personal issues Sarah's death has triggered with staff.

At the afternoon meeting with the principal, discussion focuses on the after school staff meeting and how to end this horrific day in an up beat manner. The stress of this day and thoughts of days ahead is beginning to tell on both the principal and the crisis team leader. Professionalism prevails and an outline for the staff meeting is developed. Again, it is important that Mary be in charge of the staff meeting. Roles of the team leader and the principal are finalized and both wish that it were 3:30 p.m. already.

During the afternoon it becomes evident that some students are concerned for their personal safety and fear that if they go home they may be murdered like Sarah. Near panic is exhibited by a few students as the afternoon dismissal time nears. Team members, checking their notes of information provided throughout the day by school staff, struggle to determine which students may truly be at risk. Some parents are contacted and asked to come to the school to visit with a member of the crisis team and pick up their child. Four cases of child abuse have already been uncovered throughout the day and the proper authorities have been notified. A staff member remarks that it's amazing what can happen when six pairs of trained ears come into a school setting. It is also amazing that some people, both young and old, will share some deep secrets with people they are meeting for the first time.

"It's time to put away our materials and get the room cleaned up," Sarah's teacher says as she reflects on a day, like none other, in her teaching experience. The two crisis team members who were in the room at the beginning of the day have returned to assist her. As the students file out of the room with their letters to take home, many of them exchange hugs of reassurance with the teacher and the team members. There are frowns and smiles. Some students are unusually reserved, while others are their normal selves and appearing as if nothing unusual has taken place.

Three short rings of the bell calls the staff together for the after school meeting. Mary compliments the staff on the way they handled the day. She asks how everyone is doing. Like the students, there are frowns and smiles but no tears. It appears that everyone is emotionally drained.

The crisis team leader hands out an alphabetized list of the students the team had talked to during the day and a list of parents who have been called. Several teachers comment on the thoroughness of the list. Two teachers note names of students not on the list for whom they are concerned. The team leader assures the teachers that the parents of these students will be contacted during the evening.

The brief meeting concludes with a review of the plan for the next day and a reminder that at times like this, staff should reach out to one another for support. Although the meeting has officially ended, several staff members remain to visit and comfort one another.

The After School Meeting

If a tragedy occurs during the day, the after school meeting is the first opportunity for staff to collectively gather and process information. However, if the staff has attended a before school meeting, the after school meeting presents the chance to review the days events, to respond to questions and concerns, to determine staff needs and support, and to review the plan for the next day. This meeting needs to be of short duration, but the residual benefits can have long term impact.

By five o'clock agreements have been made with several parents to come to school during the evening to visit about their home situations and the reasons their children might not feel safe. Eleven home visits have been scheduled and staff assigned to follow- up.

The crisis team sits down, some for the first time in hours, to review their lists of students who have been in the crisis center during the day. Added to the list are the names of students who were considered by staff to be at risk. Plans are made to have two team members begin to telephone the parents of the students who were deemed to be at highest risk.

Counselors at the high school are contacted and arrangements are made to have three crisis team members at the high school at seven o'clock the next morning. During a conference call with the counselors, various students are discussed and plans formulated to contact parents. It is decided that two crisis team members could go to the high school that evening to assist the counselors in calling parents.

By 6:15 p.m. parents begin to arrive at the elementary school. Some are accompanied by their children. Rooms have been set up to facilitate working with parents in small groups. Child care has been arranged for preschool children. One room has been set aside for students.

Throughout the evening, more than seventy parents come to the elementary school to share concerns, listen to others, get suggestions on helping their children, support friends and students who are grieving, and to seek help in settling previous related crisis issues in their lives. The last group of parents leaves at 10:45 in the evening.

By midnight the crisis response team has debriefed the issues arising during the evening meetings and made plans to deal with individual situations. The decision is made to recon-vene the team at 6:00 the next morning to finalize the plans for the day and begin to outline issues that will need to be ad-dressed in the days and weeks ahead. Hugs are given and the weary team members head home to their families and some needed rest.

The night passes all too quickly for some and not quickly enough for others. Although all team members are on time for the early morning meeting, it is obvious that most of the team is tired and somewhat emotionally exhausted. The hot coffee and rolls Nancy remembered to bring are a welcome sight.

As Nancy reviews the outline for the day, teams members jot down notes. The team members who will be going to the high school have already made a list of students and staff they need to see, as well as made notes to help them in contacting some parents. They depart for the high school amidst words of encour-agement and with a promise to check in with Nancy around noon.

The issue of the funeral is on the agenda for the early morning meeting. Many of the parents of the elementary stu-dents are concerned about their children attending the funeral. Team members have indicated to parents the decision is be-tween themselves and their children. However, if the decision is made that their children will be attending the funeral, parents have been encouraged to attend with them.

Plans have been made to meet with the funeral director, two relatives of the family, and the pastor from the church. One of the team members, who has had additional training in this area, will ask that the funeral be held at four o'clock in the afternoon. The rationale is students and staff may feel more free to attend the funeral if they do not have to miss school. It will be pointed out at the meeting the policy of the school district is to not close school during a crisis. The funeral director and the pastor, as well as other funeral directors and pastors in the city, have been involved in previous meetings with crisis team mem-bers at less stressful times. Both the funeral director and pastor understand the need to try and direct the relatives in setting the funeral time. However, both of them know that the relatives wishes will be honored if they choose to have the funeral at a different time.

The Funeral

In the study of thanatology, funerals are referred to as concessionary rituals. Funerals tend to fall into two categories; those that help the family and those that help others, i.e., students, staff, and friends.

Funerals held during school hours can create additional problems. For example, if a staff member dies and the funeral is held during school time, it may be difficult to accommodate staff wanting to attend the funeral and still keep school in session. Schools that dismiss the entire student body for a funeral may create more problems than they solve. And if parents can't or won't accompany their student(s) to the funeral, no matter what time of day it is, other problems may arise. Plus, some parents will not allow their student(s) to attend the funeral no matter when it is, raising more possible problems. Funeral issues can substantially affect specific crisis response plans.

The members of the team assigned to work at the high school are surprised to find so few students in the halls. As they begin their meeting with the administrative team and the counseling staff, there is obvious concern that the school day is about to begin and a large number of students are absent.

Shortly after the meeting begins, an elementary principal calls. He explains that about 200 high school students are gathered on the playground at his school. He is wondering if the high school has cancelled classes for the day.

After a brief discussion, the meeting with the administrative and counseling teams is postponed. A couple of administrators and counselors and one member of the crisis team leave for the elementary school. The other team members prepare to meet with the students who are in attendance and await word from the elementary school where the large group of high school students are gathered.

Staff arrive at the elementary school to find high school students clustered in small groups outside the building. Some students are milling around aimlessly.

Jerry Mills, the elementary school principal, emerges from one of the clusters. "They say that our elementary school is the one thing they all have in common. Many of them went to different middle schools. It seems a lot of these kids are upset about a variety of things, all the way from family concerns to the murder of the student at your high school. They are really being good kids. We haven't had any problems with them. I just thought you might like to know where about 20% of your student body is."

As Jerry finishes, several students walk over to visit with the high school administrators.

"I tried to talk over some of my feelings with my parents, but they were going out for the evening and didn't have time to talk," one of the students volunteered.

"What a bummer!" responded another. "This didn't bother me until late last night when I got to thinking about my brother in the army. He and my dad had a big argument just before he left for boot camp. As mad as my dad was at him, he might have gone off the deep end and done something crazy like this. What a bummer...."

The crisis team staff person and the high school counselors are scattered across the playground talking with the students. Some students were wondering aloud why they had come over to the elementary school.

"Everyone was going and I didn't want to get left out."

"Sure beats going to algebra."

"My cousin died of cancer last month. Boy, were his folks wigged out. Hope I don't get it."

"Only thing I ever saw dead was my dog after the neighbor ran over him. I cried for three days. Guess there isn't anyone left in Bill's family to cry."

"My folks said all of the family is in heaven except their dad."

"My sister is severely handicapped and I think sometimes my folks wish she was dead."

"I remember when my baby brother was stillborn. My mom cried for a long time. I think even though there are three boys in our family, she probably wishes it would have been me that died."

"They shouldn't have school today anyway. Doesn't anybody have any respect for the dead."

"My sister was good friends with the little girl. She used to come over to our house and play once in awhile. I teased her about her blond hair. I wish I could tell her I'm sorry."

"Everybody's gonna die someday. Now they don't have to worry when it's going to happen to them."

"I've been in this divorce group for kids. Wow, you should hear some of the stories they tell. I told them the other day it didn't make no difference to me if my folks split and if it did I could always kill myself and I wouldn't have to think about it."

"Sometimes I'd like to kill my dad. He comes in my bathroom without knocking, especially right after I've taken a shower. And he's always wanting to give a big hug and kisses. The other day he used his tongue when he was kissing me. It made me sick. Mom doesn't ever say anything about it. I don't know what to do. Wish I had a lock on my bathroom door."

"Yeah, I think I'll go to the funeral. I wonder what a dead body looks like."

"If we can hang around here until after second period, I won't have to take one of Mr. Clark's stupid biology tests. I swear, I don't know where he gets some of those questions."

Counselors, administrators, and the crisis team member finish talking with most of the students and the majority of the students disband and begin to leave for the high school. Some continue to linger, seeming not to comprehend the events that have transpired. Eventually, all of the high school students vacate the elementary school playground and the team returns to the high school.

On the trip back, the high school administrators, counselors and crisis team members make notes on some of their discussions with the students. These notes will assist them in remembering several of the issues that have been presented and will serve as a reminder to follow-up with individual students.

"Sure glad we added spiral notebooks to the crisis packets," comments a crisis team member. "It used to be that we made notes on scraps of paper or anything else we could find. At least we have a standard way and a common set of instructions to keep track of student issues and concerns."

The remainder of the morning at the high school is routine. The counselors and crisis team members work with students on an individual and small group basis. Parent calls are returned and follow-up initiated on the high school students who expressed concerns on the playground at the elementary school.

The crisis team staff at Sarah Carmichael's elementary school have also had a full morning. A large number of parents have called expressing concern for their children and requesting help in dealing with home situations. Issues unrelated to Sarah's death are surfacing. Students, parents, and staff are sharing personal experiences. Many are remembering earlier losses. Team members work to hear feelings, acknowledge guilt, lend support, and calm worries. As early afternoon approaches, the general routine of school begins to show its positive effect. Available time is used to respond to parents and do more detailed follow-up with a small number of students.

The Unrelated Issues

In times of tragedy, add up the number of students in your school, the number of certified/classified staff, the number of parents/grandparents, and depending on the situation, the number of people in your community. The total of all of these is the potential for the number of unrelated issues that can impact the situation.

One of the more difficult factors of crisis response is unrelated issues. Unrelated issues can be triggered through previous losses, school or community politics, proposed memorials, previous school practices used to handle crisis, or mismanagement of the current crisis. Like a runaway eighteen wheeler, unrelated issues can be unexpected and require a change of course in the crisis response.

Dismissal brings excitement and laughter. The level of noise in the halls is "music" to the trained ears. Conversations focus on soccer, basketball, dance, family events, after school activities, and hunger.

The mood among staff is more positive and discussions about payday gatherings, curriculum meetings, up coming vacation plans, and sales in local stores signal both emotional exhaustion and a genuine relief that children and adults are beginning to rebound from the shock of Sarah's death.

The entire crisis team convenes at 4:00 p.m. to review the events of the day, assign parent follow-up, debrief student issues, and plan strategies for the upcoming funeral.

Three team members volunteer to attend the funeral for the Carmichael family. Response options to varying events that may occur at the funeral are discussed. The team members will sit in the rear of the church. They will closely observe students and staff during and after the funeral. Both the high school and elementary principal have assigned a staff member to sit with the team members to assist team members in identifying students or staff who appear to be having unusual difficulty during or after the funeral.

At 5:30 p.m. the crisis team members leave for home. Their team responsibilities for the day will end after they have completed phone calls to parents. Some will still be talking with parents until after 11:00 p.m. Many will complete lesson plans for the next day and make calls to rearrange personal schedules. Most will feel a sense of accomplishment for their work over the past two days. A few will vow to resign their team duties after the events surrounding this tragedy are played out. All will hope this is the last time they will have to deal with a tragedy of this magnitude. None will know there are still difficult days ahead.

The Care of Response Teams

Crisis response teams usually consist of five or six school district staff members per team who have been trained to assist in times of school tragedy. In addition to responding to a crisis, the obligations of teams members may include frequent practice sessions, speaking at staff and community meetings on the topic of crisis response, meeting with representatives of the media, hospitals, law enforcement, various city/county staffs, and clergy.

Experience has shown team members frequently have "after response" issues that impact them and may impact their relationships with family and friends. Team members may need professional help in resolving these issues and to keep them from experiencing burnout.

Chapter 1

Crisis Response Teams

Selection of a Crisis Team

As schools plan how to respond to tragedies, one of the first necessities is to identify staff who can help when "bad things happen." Selecting the right people to work on a crisis team is critical to success in dealing with tragedies and moving the school, as quickly as possible, back to routine.

Schools should develop district wide crisis response teams. That is, depending on the size of the school district, members of the crisis response team should be selected from a cross section of the district. They can be certified or classified staff.

Crisis teams should be representative of staff—kindergarten through high school. All too often, schools establish separate elementary and secondary crisis teams. The thinking is that should something happen at the secondary level, the secondary team would handle the situation. Likewise, an elementary team or teams would respond to situations in elementary schools. In small school districts—the majority of schools in America—this kind of planning can cause additional problems.

Suppose, for example, that a high school student dies in a small school district. If the district has established a secondary team to respond to high school tragedies, then the school would probably have to use some of the high school staff to respond to the crisis. This means that substitutes would need to be hired to replace the staff who are serving on the team. Thus, many of the high school students would not have their regular teachers on one of the days they need them the most. This same scenario applies to a tragedy at the elementary level.

Schools should have both elementary and secondary staff serving on the same team. The major criteria for team selection should not be at which grade level someone works, but how effective that individual would be as a team member. One caution: I have found most elementary staff members can be effective team members whether they are working with elementary or secondary students. However, a secondary staff member who has not "sat on the floor and visited" with kindergarten and primary age students may feel uncomfortable with children of that age. Secondary team members should have the chance to work with young children *before* there is a crisis. Kindergarten and primary teachers will welcome them in their classrooms to read to students and have the opportunity to get to know how young minds work. It can save a lot of sweaty palms in the long run.

Frequently, school administrators are the ones who select staff to serve on crisis teams. There are six factors to keep in mind when making these selections.

1. Involve school staff in making suggestions as to who should be on the team.
2. Ask questions like, "If we were to have a tragedy, who on the staff would be calm? If you had a personal problem, who on the staff would you feel comfortable sharing it with? When we are faced with problem situations, which staff members seem to always have the most practical solutions? Who on the staff communicates well, verbally or in writing, with other staff, students, and the community?"
3. Select staff who have a sincere desire to serve on a team.
4. Select staff who can respect sensitive information and maintain confidentiality.
5. Select those who have the trust and respect of others, including colleagues, administration, and the board of education.
6. Remember, educational background and training are not the major criteria for team selection.

Administrators as Team Members

One of the advantages of crisis response teams is their ability to bring five to six trained individuals into a school and to effectively deal with a tragedy that is impacting students and staff. Seldom are all students or staff affected the same way by a school tragedy.

However, no matter the magnitude of the impact upon the staff and students, it is important that school administration focus their attention on the entire school and not just the crisis situation.

Schools always need good leadership. Never is that more true than during a tragedy. Therefore, careful thought should be given to the inclusion of administrators serving on crisis response teams.

I'm reminded of the principal who telephoned to explain a situation in his school. A 16-year-old student had been killed in a car/train accident. The young woman was a junior in high school and had attended school in her community since kindergarten. This principal had participated in a training workshop. He called to report that although he remembered not all students might be affected by the crisis, he was still surprised that of the 243 high school's students, only 19 had signed out to go to the funeral. Of those, he said, only 13 actually attended the funeral. The other 6 drove to another community and ate pizza.

His major dilemma was that even the 13 students who attended the funeral did not return to school, but chose to go to one of the student's homes and watch videos. As a result "the attendance book" showed 19 students were truant for either all or part of the day. As he concluded his story and the various issues he had to deal with, it was obvious he was truly surprised and disappointed at the small number of students who actually attended the young woman's funeral.

If this administrator had been a member of his school district's crisis team, my guess is the number of students who were affected by the young woman's death would have been greater. If the building administrator is the leader of the school, educationally and otherwise, what happens to the school when the administrator, as a crisis team member, directs that leadership and skills to a limited population of the students and staff? How can a school maintain a semblance of routine and hope to rapidly return to a collective routine if the building leader, i.e., the principal, is unable to respond to daily routine items as well as crisis issues? One way to cause more and more students and staff to be impacted by a crisis is to limit the role of the principal to crisis response only.

Another reason school administrators should not serve directly on crisis response teams is because of the "do you think this would be OK" factor. All too often, crisis response teams who have administrators serving on them have team members who have a tendency to seek approval of their plans and actions from the administrator on the team. Because of the time honored tradition of checking matters out with an administrator, team members tend to function less creatively and often seem limited by the administrator's paradigm of crisis management.

School administrators can serve the school best by managing the school routine during a tragedy and letting the crisis response team manage the tragedy. Are administrators left out of the crisis plans? Do administrators not have input? Does the crisis response team take over the school? The answer to these questions is a resounding *no.* Crisis response teams make the plans, the administrator approves them. Crisis response teams seek administrator input after they have used their training and expertise as a team in developing the best plan for the situation. Administrators have the final decision regarding the plan of action. Crisis response teams are there to support the administrator, students, and staff, not take over the school. There must be a combined effort by the team and the school administrator. They must work together if the entire school community is to benefit and the students and staff are to receive the kind of support and assistance they need and deserve.

Counselors as Crisis Team Members

Some people believe that counselors, because of their unique training, are the logical choice to serve on a crisis response team. Many school counselors do make excellent crisis team members. They are good listeners and understand the needs of students who are in shock or grief. Counselor training provides today's school counselors with the opportunity to learn specific skills that help students and staff during a time of tragedy.

Many school districts make the mistake, however, in assuming because school counselors have this unique training, they automatically make good crisis team members. That may not always be the case. Crisis team members must be interested in serving on a team, must have the support of the staff, must be team players, must maintain confidentiality, must be calm and use common sense during times of tragedies, and must be able to work effectively with all age levels of students. These criteria are applied to *all* who are being considered as crisis team members, including counselors.

School Psychologists as Crisis Team Members

Another valuable human resource for crisis response teams may be the school psychologist. Like counselors, many school psychologists have training in helping people during times of extreme stress.

School psychologists are usually itinerate and, all too often, they are spread across a number of schools, sometimes even in more than one school district. But again, the same team selection criteria must be applied. If school psychologists meet the criteria for team selection, their immediate availability and the length of time they can remain committed to a specific event may be the determining factor in their selection as team members.

Teachers as Crisis Response Team Members

What about teachers as crisis response team members? Daily, many teachers deal, not only with the subject matter they are assigned to deliver, but with the complexity of issues and concerns that confront their students. As a group, teachers are caring and alert to the needs of students; therefore, they are logical resources to tap when seeking individuals who will be effective crisis team members.

If teachers are selected to serve on your district wide crisis response team, try to select staff from both elementary and secondary levels. Teachers may need some "practice" in working with different students, i.e., elementary with secondary and secondary with elementary, before a tragedy presents itself in your school district.

Teachers who serve on crisis response teams must be available to leave their assigned classrooms during the time the crisis response team has been activated. School administrators must be prepared to bring in a substitute teacher on a moment's notice or cover the classroom until a substitute arrives to assume the teacher's duties.

Nurses as Crisis Response Team Members

Health professionals can make excellent crisis response team members. Frequently school tragedies are the result of accidents. When this happens, the local medical community, i.e., hospitals, doctors, and emergency personnel, are usually involved. It is at this time that a nurse, serving on a crisis response team or serving as a consultant to a team, can be of immense value.

The school nurse may be able to obtain information from the hospital that can be very helpful in determining how the crisis response team will structure their responses. If, for example, a student has been hospitalized as a result of an accident, the nurse may be the only person outside of the student's immediate family who can obtain accurate and sometimes private information from the hospital staff or the attending physicians. Up to date and accurate information can prove invaluable in structuring a crisis response.

In a school system which had a trained crisis response team, a student was struck by a car after school hours and rushed to the hospital. The response team was called early in the evening and met shortly thereafter to make plans for the next school day. Although the student was listed in critical condition, the team was unable to obtain accurate information as to the nature of the injuries and the prognosis.

A call by a school nurse to the attending physician revealed the student had severe head trauma. The prognosis was guarded and the response team was able to use that information to plan a multistage response. When the team received word early the next morning that the student had died, it was able to move ahead with the portion of the plan developed for just such an outcome. The result was a well planned and executed response to the students and staff.

Classified Staff as Crisis Team Members

Criteria for selection of crisis team members usually does not preclude the use of classified staff as team members. Bus drivers, custodians, school secretaries, school cafeteria employees, crossing guards, and para-educators have been trained as team members. Some turned out to be excellent crisis response team members, providing just the right insight and skills to compliment certified staff on the team.

Classified staff can bring a different perspective to the crisis response team and make response suggestions that address issues or concerns certified staff may not consider. Classified staff may have ties to the community that are very helpful in shaping an effective response.

Using Non-School Staff as Crisis Team Members

Schools may or may not use non-school staff on crisis response teams. However, experience with schools across the nation suggests it is better to use school personnel. The vast majority of these people have demonstrated a strong commitment to working with young people. They are intelligent, well educated, caring adults who have chosen to labor in our schools. And, with proper training, a high percent of them would make excellent crisis response team members.

The question, then, seems to be why use non-school people to work on crisis response teams when there is such an excellent resource of people currently working for the schools? Several answers present themselves.

One is a lack of confidence by administrators. Some schools say, "What do we know about this kind of stuff, let's bring in some outside professionals."

Granted, there are a number of well-qualified professionals in the community ready and willing, but not necessarily able, to assist schools during times of crisis. These people, such as private practice psychologists and other mental health professionals, all practice in the mental health arena, but they may not understand the daily operation of schools. Having attended school is not a viable condition for understanding the complexity of today's schools. All too frequently, people who do not work directly with schools are unaware of the nuances of change that have taken place in America's schools.

The majority of today's mental health professionals are in business to make a profit. Even non profit mental health organizations usually must generate dollars to survive. On some occasions, schools have reported outside professionals have followed up with the families whose students they accessed during a crisis and recommended the family become involved in private therapy. Sometimes this may be appropriate. But, the school has, in effect, given a few private practitioners chances to recruit business in the schools.

Now, let's suppose you are not one of the private mental health practitioners who was asked to assist the school during its time of need. The "uninvited," so to speak, write letters to the local board of education, the local newspapers and make public comments at board meetings.

This same thinking applies to using clergy, especially in public schools, to either serve on response teams or to assist the school in times of tragedy. Here again, the stage may be set for the creation of another problem.

As educators know, and as the U.S. Constitution declares, there is a separation of church and state. People have a right to chose or not chose religion. Therefore, permitting members of the clergy to work in schools during times of crisis may create overriding issues that complicate the situation. Mental health professionals and clergy have their place in helping students, staff, and communities address a tragedy. They may play an even more important role in the healing process. The issue is whether they can be most effective within the walls of our schools or most effective in their private offices, churches and synagogues, and people's homes. Excluding clergy and mental health professionals from a crisis team is not an easy decision for some schools to make.

A final thought regarding the use of outside staff in managing school tragedy is the message that it sends to the community. Frequently it is a message of inadequacy. Patrons in the community get mixed messages when schools call in outside help. All too often the message is that school personnel can not handle the situation because they do not have the ability and are not prepared to manage crises when they arise.

On the contrary, our schools have qualified personnel. They are a valuable resource that should not be wasted or overlooked. They can provide the assistance students, staff members, and parents need. Select appropriate staff members, offer them proper training, give them strong support, and they will validate the decision to use school-based crisis response teams.

Selection of appropriate staff to serve on a crisis response team is an essential ingredient in the total recipe that makes a successful team. But, as the saying goes, there is no greater burden than having potential. In the final analysis it is training and team building that will form those individuals into an effective team that will take a school staff and students to a successful conclusion of a tragedy.

Team Building

The best way to build a close knit and effective crisis response team is to have them respond to a school tragedy. That is, unfortunately, also the worst way because of the real-life suffering.

After you have selected your team members, they need time to work together and develop a working relationship. The importance of time spent together can not be over emphasized. Too often teams are selected and the first time they have the opportunity to meet one another is when they are responding to a very stressful situation. Because they do not know each other very well, the team members may not work efficiently and they might have a difficult time "healing themselves" after responding to a crisis.

Because crisis response teams usually consist of five or six members, it is useful to select two alternates to serve on the team. This allows team members the flexibility they need to be effective. Vacations, illness, personal situations, and other issues may come into play when a crisis occurs. The alternates, who also train and work with the team, are valuable resources and support to the team concept.

One way to develop team cohesiveness is to have the team practice with hypothetical cases and scenarios. This work gives team members experience in resolving problems they may confront as well as the opportunity to learn about and gain respect for individual team member's skills. Scenarios can be created by simply reading about a crisis in the national news or perhaps listing potential tragedies that could occur in your school setting because of its size and geographical location. Be creative and explore all possibilities.

All too often the first comment by schools wanting advice on how to handle a particular situation is, "We never thought anything like this could happen in our school." Common practice scenarios could include: accidental death of a student or staff member, student suicide, terminal illness of a staff person or student, or some sort of disaster in the community that affects the school district. Uncommon scenarios, yet ones that could occur in any school, could include: a staff member with AIDS, a staff member accused of molesting students, the rape of a student or staff member in the school building or on the school campus, a bus accident involving a bus driver under the influence of alcohol or other drugs, students and/or staff being held hostage, food poisoning from school cafeteria meals, multiple suicides, and the shooting of a student or staff member by another student or staff member. All of these and more have happened in our nation's schools. Have your teams practice and prepare. Remember the old adage about an once of prevention....

Team building and cohesiveness is also developed as the team members begin to know the backgrounds, both professional and personal, of individual team members. Some of the most effective crisis response teams are comprised of groups of people who share their worries and concerns. All of us have had experiences in our lives that profoundly affect our ability to respond to certain situations. As team members develop trust and respect for each other, they usually are more willing to discuss the events in their lives that may affect them during a crisis response.

At a recent crisis response team training session, one of the team members began to cry during one of the scenario exercises. The team member shared a fear of having to respond to the death of a kindergarten or first grade student. She told of a recent death of her young grandchild and that responding to the death of a young student rekindled unpleasant memories. The other team members listened intently and were very supportive of their team member. What resulted was the sharing of a series of personal hurts that various team members had experienced. The end result was a group of individuals who, through shared experiences and empathy for each other's feelings, became a strong team ready to respond to a crisis and support one another as they collectively mustered up the energy to reach out and help others in time of need.

Team Acceptance by Staff/Employees

"Why were you selected and I wasn't?" "I think all that crisis stuff would be interesting." "I know how people feel when they have had a loss."

Unfortunately, crisis teams can receive negative reactions from some certified and classified staff. This reaction is common when teams have not explained what the crisis team members do during times of tragedy. Too often the first exposure a staff gets to the team is when a tragedy has happened and emotions are running high. Response teams, after they have developed a general response plan and it has been approved by the administrative staff, should schedule a meeting with all certified and classified staff. At this meeting the team is introduced. They explain the general plan and review procedures, i.e., special meeting times, the rationale for a crisis room for adults and students, and basic information that would be available at a staff meeting during a crisis. If your school uses substitute staff, they should be asked to attend this meeting. The meeting should offer time for questions and school administrators should be in attendance at the meeting. An administrator may wish to begin the meeting with a few comments and introductions, but members of the crisis response team should make the presentation.

If your district has several buildings or sites, it is best to make presentations at each building rather than have a large staff meeting. Staff are usually more comfortable meeting in their own building with their peers. In order to give the teams more exposure, team members may need to divide up to make these presentations. However, at least two team members should make each presentation. These presentations can also be scheduled over a period of days or weeks to allow the team members to work together.

Although all staff members will not remember the specifics of what the response team does, most will remember they did attend some type of presentation. In the event of a crisis, don't expect staff be able to locate any of the materials handed out at the initial meeting. Be certain you have sufficient copies of the response plan and any additional materials available when the team is on an actual response. Each year you may have new employees that need to be included in an informational meeting or as part of a staff orientation.

If you have gone to the work of organizing a snappy presentation, delivered it, but still feel that some are not sold on the idea of crisis response, try to relax! Most staff will be appreciative and work cooperatively during or shortly after your response to a crisis in their building. Some will particularly have more appreciation and be supportive when routine is established in the school. A few may never admit, at least publicly, the team was helpful. Take your gains as a team and move on. After all, the primary purpose is to assist those students and staff who acknowledge the need for help. There will be plenty of these.

Working with Boards, Patrons, and the Community

Most organizations have some type of governing body. Schools across this nation are locally controlled and operated by a board whose responsibility is setting policy. If your district is to have a viable, comprehensive response when tragedy visits your school district, your board must know in advance what the basic response plan entails. In some districts, the most difficult part of a crisis response is positioning yourself with the board.

Generally speaking, the district's spokesperson to the board is the superintendent. It goes without saying, if the superintendent is not supportive of the need for a response team that uses defined procedures, there can be problems in getting board support.

Fortunately, with proper training, planning, and a dash of political savvy, most teams do not encounter substantial opposition at the board level. There are, however, some specific strategies that are helpful.

1. Make certain your administrative team, especially the superintendent, is supportive of the concept of crisis response.
2. Make certain all administrators are comfortable with the selection process for team members.
3. Make certain the administrative team has reviewed the general response plan and has had sufficient opportunity for input.
4. Make certain the administrative team has signed off on the plan and that it has 100% of their support.
5. Make certain the response team(s) are in attendance at the board meeting when the plan is presented.

Ideally, the superintendent should introduce the general concept of crisis response and introduce the team members. Members of the team should explain the plan to the board and assist the superintendent in responding to questions.

The concept of response and an outline of the basic plan are generally presented at this informational session with the board. Keep the presentation simple and avoid involvement in a dialogue with the board on "what if's," i.e., what would be the plan if the school burned down, what would be the plan if we had a hostage situation, if a teacher was sexually assaulted, and if a 747 hit the building. Try to make the point that you are presenting a general concept of response and a general plan outlining procedures. The specifics will be developed in response to each event and will be based on the situation that presents itself.

Normally it is not necessary for boards to approve the general plan. The key is they are aware staff has been trained to successfully handle crisis situations and there are general plans in place to cover almost any crisis event.

Patrons

More than one crisis team has had difficulty because they did not do their homework with the parents of the students they serve. Not only do you need to be diligent in working successfully with staff, students, and board members, you must organize communication efforts with the patrons of your district.

As with staff, the time to present information to parents is *before* grief comes to visit. PTO's/PTA's are good places to begin. Volunteer to present at meetings and respond to questions and concerns. The majority of the parents will be supportive of the school district's foresight in planning for tragic events. It's not unusual for a significant percent of those attending the meeting to have had grief/crisis experiences when they were younger. Use caution in allowing much, if any, sharing from the past. Not only can it get out of control, it has the potential to lead the discussion into areas that may erode your chances of a successful meeting.

The presentation should be well planned, keeping in mind you are talking to lay people. It should be written so the person living across the street from the school can understand it. Translated, that means avoid the use of educational jargon, i.e., crisis response team, crisis rooms, and Post Traumatic Stress Syndrome. This type of language may only serve to raise the parents' level of concern.

Your job in this presentation is to assure parents that the school district has developed a broad plan to help students, staff, and parents during tragic events that may divert the school from its main mission—instruction. Assure them you will keep them informed (later we will discuss designing letters to be sent home to parents) and your team(s) have the necessary expertise to handle any situation that may arise.

At this point someone in the audience may volunteer their services and attempt to lead the discussion toward using parents during times of crisis. The parent will be sincere and may even have some expertise in this field. Of course, you have anticipated this situation and immediately show your audience an overlay that clearly demonstrates the need for parents to help their children at home. Parents will thereby be reassured they do have a very important role to play and the meeting moves on to a successful conclusion.

Another way to inform parents is through a series of home meetings. These meetings are usually organized by members of the school's parent group. Although the number of people at each meeting may vary, it is another opportunity to inform parents of the school's proactive approach to crisis. The fact that team members are on the "parent's turf" lends itself to a more informal meeting than a meeting at school.

No matter where you hold meetings for your patrons, keys for success include:

1. Demonstrate the preparedness of the response team.

2. Present the crisis plan.

3. Assure parents you will help them help their student(s).

4. Present rationale for not having certain types of memorials. (See Chapter 14.)

5. If necessary, give examples of local or regional resources that can help students with long term follow-up.

6. Remind them their church, if they attend one, can be a resource and support but assure them religious issues are not a part of the school's response effort.

7. Emphasize if the crisis event involves the death of a student or staff member that families need to decide if their student should attend the funeral. Reinforce the need for adults to attend funerals with their students *no matter the student's age.*

8. Respond to questions.

9 Smile, thank everyone, and leave.

Community

All too often, educators forget only about 30% to 55% of the people in the community may have school age children. This oversight can be detrimental in the successful campaign of a school bond or tax levy issue and it can hinder the school's response to a tragic event. History reminds us rumor and innuendo have brought down many a powerful house. But, with foresight and some work, crisis teams can significantly cut their losses and garner community support for their efforts.

A proven way to inform communities about the work of crisis teams is to get on the service club speaker's circuit. Most service clubs are always looking for someone or some group to present a twenty to twenty-five minute program. The rules for crisis team presentations to staff and parents also apply here. But, there are additional circumstances that need to be considered.

You will have a mixture of parents and those in the community who never had or no longer have children in school. Your presentation should be a basic one, keeping in mind there will be varying levels of interest and understanding. If possible, use examples of recent school crisis events presented in the media. If there have been tragic events in your community or surrounding communities, point to them.

If appropriate, point out these teams serve for no pay and, in effect, the taxpayers are getting more "bang for their buck." Emphasize learning is the primary goal of the school and response teams are trained to more effectively help students with grief issues so they can move back to learning. Remind them routine is important in the lives of young people. Hammer home the concept that schools, through proper planning, can frequently minimize the number of students who are "caught up" in the event.

Because team members usually have a short time for their presentation, avoid the issue of religion and memorials unless they come up in the question/answer part of the presentation. Expect some of the club members to visit with team members after the presentation and pursue more specific information on these and other topics.

Another way to convey your message to the community at large is through the media. The crisis team will have an excellent opportunity to do this when they meet with representatives from the media for practice sessions. (See Chapter 3)

If you have your choice, the print media is the best way to tell your story to the general public. Radio and television are less effective unless members of the team are on a talk show or have the opportunity to be on a half hour program devoted to one subject.

Assuming that you choose to use a newspaper or magazine to tell your team's story, organize your presentation and spend time anticipating the nature of the questions the reporter will ask. Put yourself in their position and think through what you would want to know if you were a reporter writing the story. You can never be misquoted on radio or television, but you can be taken out of context. On the other hand, the print media can misquote you. So, be concise, clear, and provide them with written information that will help them better understand what school crisis teams are all about. Ask them if it would be possible to read the article before it is published.

Your community can be anyone out there who has an interest, positive or negative, about public school educations. Your team will have opportunities to prove their worth when, for example, they meet with local morticians, law enforcement personnel, and hospital staffs. Use every opportunity to tell your story. It will pay dividends in the long run.

Mock Training for Various Situations

Practice makes perfect. For those of you who are 4.0 or better tennis players or play to a 3 or better golf handicap, you may have trouble understanding how most of us struggle to do some things well. Talent comes into "play" in many of the things we do and do well in our lives. Collective talent and practice frequently make the difference in successfully responding to tragedies.

In a more perfect world, crisis teams would not exist. In the real world, however, these teams not only exist but must perform and perform well. Granted, crisis teams usually are much better after their first response. The first response, big or small, gives them an opportunity to put training into practice. More importantly, this first response gives them a chance to critique their work, access their mental toughness, get rid of some of the butterflies, and realize tragedy does not always happen somewhere else.

It would be of little comfort to you, however, if local fire department members, after losing your house to a fire, said the experience gave them the opportunity to critique their work, access their mental toughness, get rid of some of the butterflies, and realize tragedy does not always happen somewhere else. Just like the fire department, crisis response teams need to do it right the first time. *Practice!*

School crisis teams should meet on a regular basis to review procedures, reacquaint themselves with other team members, receive additional training, and practice. Each team meeting should include fifteen to twenty minutes for the team to work on a crisis scenario. Team members should take turns sharing the responsibility of developing the practice session. This responsibility may go to the team leader, but all members should have the opportunity to think up scenarios.

The following are suggestions for developing practice scenarios.

1. Keep the practice short, generally 15 to 20 minutes. This will keep your team focused and help the team develop the skills to work quickly and effectively.

2. Be practical but creative. Develop scenarios that are likely to happen in your school(s) and community, keeping in mind this can be a wild and crazy world.

3. Be flexible. Design scenarios that cover a variety of issues from death and accidents to food poisoning, i.e., school cafeteria tacos that make half of the student body ill, or hostage situations.

4. If you are running low on ideas, check the newspaper or watch a national news telecast. If possible, practice working with the media and include them in one of your practice sessions.

5. Include the unexpected in the practice scenarios. Half way through the session add information that requires a change in the design of the response. Require team members to be flexible in their thinking and work under pressure. Help them work within a time constraint.

6. Practice responding to community interests and well-intended, but less than helpful, actions. What will the team do when members of the clergy show up at school and expect to be involved? What if a popular mental health professional in the community goes on television and volunteers his or her expertise? Suppose a group of well meaning parents want to work with students in the crisis room and arrive unannounced. Suppose seventy percent of the student body walk out in the middle of a response and the crisis team is pressured to split up and go to the various homes, parking lots, and restaurants were the students have gathered. Be sure to include a variety of problems in the practice sessions.

7. Don't set your crisis team(s) up for failure. If you ask young children to describe what they think would be appropriate punishment for a rule infraction at home, they frequently come up with much more severe punishment than the parent had in mind. The same can be true in designing scenarios. Sometimes the practice scenarios go way beyond what may conceivably happen. Balance your practice with easy, moderate, and difficult situations. Teams can lose their confidence because they could not figure out solutions to nearly impossible scenarios. Sometimes in the middle of a real crisis response, there are not very good solutions for some of the problems that arise.

By practicing regularly, you will not only be better prepared when tragedy strikes, but you will also reap the side benefits: team building, confidence, a calm presence, and a broad repertoire of skills. Practice may not make perfect, but it beats the alternative which all too often is confusion, lack of team cohesiveness, personal anxiety, and limited skills.

Are there basic tenets in crisis response? Are there general procedures that can be followed? Is there a method for a successful response? The answer to all of these is a resounding *yes.*

The basic recipe for a successful crisis response includes:

1. An active well trained team with the skills to respond to all age and grade levels.

2. An organized and effective system for notifying crisis team members that a crisis has occurred.

3. A system for notifying staff, certified and classified, of the crisis. These people should already have been involved in a brief in-service on the district's general plan for crisis response.

4. A general plan for crisis response that has been developed *prior* to a crisis event.

5. An immediate and quick development of a specific plan focused on the crisis at hand.

Implementing these five basic ingredients into your school's response to a crisis will insure a more acceptable resolution of the situation and will more quickly return your school(s) to their primary mission of directing student learning.

After Thoughts

Successfully responding to a crisis in a school is difficult, at best. Sometimes it may border on the impossible. Even though crisis teams may have capable and experienced members, even though school staff members have confidence in the team of people responding to the school crisis event, even though the students in the school are receptive to the assistance the crisis team is giving them, and even though the parents and school patrons are supportive of the school's efforts in responding to the crisis, sometimes it just doesn't go as planned.

But, what if the reason "things" do not go as planned is because some team members do not pull their weight, because some of the school staff do not think that certain members of the crisis response are very competent, because some of the school's administrative team do not have total confidence in the crisis response team, because many students impacted by the crisis event do not seem to be receiving appropriate assistance from team members; or because parents do not respond positively to efforts of the school's crisis response team?

Although lots of thought (some if it in this chapter) has been given to a foolproof recipe for concocting the best mix of people that would constitute an ideal school crisis response, sometimes the results do not meet the intended outcome. Members of school crisis response teams are, after all, human. They have good days and not so good days. They have personal and professional priorities distracting their focus. They have crisis events in their lives that preclude their ability, at times, to respond to a school crisis appropriately, let alone successfully. They have children of their own and are reminded that the students they are responding to could just as well have been their children. They have skills, but they are only mere mortals. They have training, but they become distracted. They have positive attitudes, but they can be negative. They have a love for kids, but not for all of them. They have great crisis response talent, but they can lose interest. Stuff happens! (Or something like that.)

In this age of digital cameras, you might get the idea that if you don't like the image you have captured, it can simply be erased. That may be true in the world of high-tech cameras, but not in the world of school crisis response. It is not that easy to erase the picture of a chaotic or ill-fated response to an emergency or crisis in a school or school district. Elephants are not the only "animals" with long memories.

So, one might ask, is there a magic formula for school crisis response that will take into account the diversity of those individuals willing to reach out to students and staff during really difficult and disruptive times? After all, in most school districts, school crisis team members receive no additional pay for their service on a team and little if any appreciation for their efforts. Most of the time they receive little if any assistance in helping themselves manage their emotions during and after school crisis events. In most districts, school crisis team members are taken from their main jobs in the district, work extended hours, handle stressful and emotional events, work to the point of exhaustion, and then return to their "regular jobs" and make up all the work they missed or have to straighten out the problems resulting from their absence. Whew!

There may not be a magic formula for school crisis response, but some things do work better than others in putting together a team or teams of individuals capable of designing an effective, proactive, and successful response to a crisis in a school district or individual school building. As school districts organize school crisis teams, they may want to consider learning from the mistakes of others:

- Make certain there is one team leader for each team. Good leadership is difficult to find and maintain. Although members of the crisis team may have marvelous skills, few members of the team usually have marvelous *leadership* skills. Find a good team leader and stick with that person. (See page 53 for a job description for a crisis team leader.)

- Not all people who volunteer to be on a school crisis response team should be on the team. Those responsible for selecting team members must be willing to make difficult decisions. One of those decisions may be to graciously decline a person's offer to serve.

- Individual's familiar with schools of the 21st century, who are capable and comfortable working in school settings during highly stressful and even frightening events, should be recruited for school crisis response.

- Politics are a part of effective school crisis response. Select politically astute people for service on crisis teams. "Rough seas" will need to be sailed during times of crisis. Don't recruit or select crisis team members who do not have "sea legs" or those who have a penchant toward "sea sickness."

- "Loose lips sink ships" (following the sea theme). More than one school crisis team's ship has sunk as a result of team members sharing inappropriate and sensitive information outside the ranks of the crisis team. Do not select people for crisis teams who have a history, penchant or, if possible, any potential to share information outside the team.

- Practice makes perfect. School crisis team members need to meet on a regular basis and practice. With practice comes skill; and with skill comes confidence. School crisis teams will need both. With practice also can come a level of comfort among team members. That level of comfort can be invaluable during an anxiety filled crisis event.

- Avoid "school crisis team clubs." Although school districts want their crisis team members to work well together, know each other's skills, and have team building experiences, they do not need a crisis team "club." By their very nature, clubs limit membership and denote exclusivity. Although friendships and camaraderie may evolve between some members of a school crisis team, teams and team members should strive to avoid the image of "those people" or "that group." And special tee shirts or hats— NO!

Job description for a school crisis team leader

- Organized crisis team training for team members.
- Responsible for crisis team public relations.
- Convening team for crisis response.
- Liaison with the school districts administrative team.
- Spokesperson to school patrons and the community.
- Knowing and appropriately using the skills of team members.
- Contact person with other school crisis team leaders in the geographical area.
- Knows when to step aside and lay down the reigns of leadership.
- Knows significant events going on in the lives of other team members.
- Is a role model for other crisis team members.
- Has "a life" outside the world of school crisis response.
- Has a working knowledge of crisis response resources in the community.

Chapter 2

The General Plan

Assuming that your school district has trained teams and there is a system in place (i.e., calling tree, pagers) to alert the team that their services are needed, let's examine what a general crisis plan looks like. Remember, this is the general plan for response. Every individual response will require a specific plan for each unique situation, and they will all be unique.

Begin your general plan manual with an overview or purpose. An example would be:

The purpose of this manual is to provide staff with a quick reference guide to use in a crisis. It is the _____ (name of organization) philosophy that a planned and organized approach is more effective in reducing psychological and social difficulties following a crisis. This Crisis Response Manual includes procedures that were designed to deal with a number of tragedies that could occur in _____ (name of organization). These procedures do not cover every condition that might develop and it may not always be possible to follow every procedural step. This manual can be used in conjunction with _____ .(Specify other materials and plans that may exist.)

The crisis manual should be broken down into parts that cover specific areas and as many checklists as possible should be used to simplify the procedures you want the staff to follow.

Various school districts have asked to have their crisis manuals reviewed. They usually preface their request with something like, "Our board of education is having difficulty understanding our crisis manual," or "Our staff is having trouble tracking the steps we want them to follow." A couple of days later their crisis manual arrives by delivery truck and you can hear the driver grunting and groaning as he struggles to carry it. The floor shakes and the windows rattle when the delivery person sets it on the counter. And the school can't figure out why people don't understand it?

Streamline your crisis manual. Your audience wants to know general procedures. They do not want nor do they need all of the details. Save those for the specific plan that is written for each event and is only seen by crisis team members and the school administrative team.

Begin the general plan with a checklist of procedures for the building administrators. Administrators often must react to and adjust to situations. That is one of the expectations of the job. They are expected to make decisions. If the administrative team has a set of procedures to follow in the early stages of a crisis event, they will generally follow them. So, write these procedures down and put them where they can find them; which is preferably in the front of the manual.

Administrative Procedures

Items that should appear on the administrative checklist include:

1. Activate the crisis response team, phone #_____
2. Inform the superintendent, phone #_____
3. Verify information regarding the crisis.
4. Activate the building calling tree. (Leave space at the end of the manual to list the calling tree.)
5. If possible, call the parent or family.
6. Call 911 for emergency services. If it is necessary to send anyone to the hospital by ambulance, send a staff member along to serve as a liaison between the hospital and the school with instructions to relay information back to the school as soon as possible.

These and other items that may apply to your situation will be helpful to administrators as well as the crisis response team. Administrators who make inappropriate decisions in the early stages of the response usually do so because they do not have any guidelines and there has not been discussion or agreement on the role of members of the administrative team. As the saying goes, "plan your work and work your plan." Take time to do it right and cover all of your bases.

Media Procedures

The staff should follow the administrative procedures section of the manual. All too often, building personnel find themselves confronted by members of the press. Building staff will have precious little time to hunt up the section of the manual that helps them handle the media. Many times excellent responses to crisis situations are not reflected in the newspaper, radio, or television coverage of the crisis. The school does a superb job of responding, but they may do a less than superb job of managing the media. Thus, they do well but look bad. The goal is to do a good job and look good at the same time. If the community, through improper handling of the media, thinks the school is not responding appropriately, this may create another crisis. Do good—look good.

About the only means to inform the general public of a school crisis is by the mass media. Therefore, it is important to ensure the media receives prompt, accurate information. Isolated quotes from individuals can be incomplete or misleading and should be avoided. Media procedures should include:

1. Determine who the building media contact person will be. (See Chapter 3 concerning specific information on managing the media and tips for interviews.)

2. Inform the office staff they may be receiving media calls and direct them as to the procedures to be followed.

3. Recommend students and staff not talk to the media.

4. *Do not* allow media personnel in the school building.

5. Notify the superintendent's office that media contact has been made.

Utilizing the Crisis Response Team

Even though the district crisis team knows what the procedures for crisis management are and how they can best be utilized, school staff may forget how to properly use a crisis response team. So, in your crisis manual, you will need a section that reminds administrators and other staff how to best utilize the services of the team.

Included in this section of the manual should be information on how to contact the crisis team. Include weekday, weekend, holiday, and summer phone numbers. If it is possible to use a twenty-four hour answering service, it will simplify the procedure for staff when they need to contact the team.

Additionally, remind staff that the crisis response team can:

1. Meet with building administrators and the staff to formulate an action plan.
2. Assist in handling media coverage.
3. Facilitate staff meetings to provide information related to the crisis.
4. Support school staff.
5. Help teachers process information with students.
6. Work with students individually or in groups.
7. Be available for contact with parents.
8. Provide helpful, factual information to parents.

This section of the manual should also include a reminder that the crisis team is a supportive service which can assess, plan, and intervene in crises affecting staff and students. Reemphasize planning and the impact an organized approach has in reducing the emotional and social impact of a crisis. Point out the special training the teams have to assist building administrators in directing crisis resolution activities.

A word of caution: Be certain to have reviewed this information with counselors in the schools. For whatever reason, some counselors may not be members of a response team and may be uncomfortable when some "strangers" come into their school and do what school counselors perceive to be counseling. Working out these issues with the building counselor(s) may keep the team from having an additional crisis when they are working in the school(s).

The Principal's Responsibilities in the Event of the Death of a Student's Parent/Guardian

The grim reaper, another euphemism for death, swings his scythe in a wide arc. Depending on the number of students and staff in your school district, multiplied by their relatives and various family situations, the potential for tragedy is significant. Because so many people can be involved, directly or indirectly, the crisis response manual should contain a plan if a student's parent or guardian dies.

A checklist for principals confronted with this crisis should contain the following suggestions:

1. Verification of the death. This can be done through the spouse, family, hospital, police, or even a mortuary.

2. Inform the student's teacher(s).

3. Inform the student's classmates and other friends. It may be necessary to coordinate with other principals/buildings that may be involved.

4. A visit to the family by appropriate school personnel, i.e., teacher, counselor, principal. Frequently people say they are reluctant to make a home visit because they are concerned about what to say to the family. Experience has shown, and this has been confirmed repeatedly by people who work in this area, the family does the majority of the talking and your primary function is to listen. Remember, depending on the situation, this is an opportunity to discuss funeral plans with the family and discreetly interject the school's position. Nothing ventured, nothing gained. (See Chapter 13.)

5. Arrange for a remembrance from the school, i.e., food, card, flowers. There is a difference between these and memorials. (See Chapter 14.)

6. Arrange for appropriate staff to attend the services. This may not be as easy as it sounds. If the funeral is after school hours, staff members attending the funeral will not be a problem. However, you may find yourself in another crisis if the funeral is during the school day. Many districts across the county require staff to take personal leave to attend funerals, especially if they are not immediate family. This can be a source of friction among the staff members. Also keep in mind you may have staff who should, for a variety of reasons, attend the funeral, but they choose not to attend—yet another delicate issue.

7. In the case of a death of a student's parent(s) or sibling(s), identify people available (counselors and crisis team members) to help the teacher talk with the student's classmates about the death and how to welcome the student back. Equipping students with some skills before a grieving classmate returns to school is essential. But don't be surprised if, for example, a student's parent dies and the student returns to school the same or next day. In some situations a student's main support system is the peer group. School staff may be caught off guard when students function outside of what the staff perceive to be an "accepted survivor paradigm."

8. Make counseling available for grieving students when they return to school. This could be counseling provided by school staff (a teacher or counselor) or, if families prefer, refer them to outside professional help. This can be a sensitive issue for families. Go slowly and remember children tend to grieve in short intervals or may have delayed grief and so kept the lines of communication open with the family.

9. Plan and provide follow-up visit(s) with the family. It is not uncommon for people who have "lost" family members through death to comment they are often treated like the dead person did not even exist. Visitors ask how they are doing, but shy away from discussions about the person who has died. Take your lead from the family, but do not hesitate to share your memories about the dead person. Avoid making comments or conclusions as to your perceptions about where you think the person(s) you're visiting with is in the grief process. Comments like, "You ought to be on stage three," referring to Kubler-Ross's stages of grief, are inappropriate. Let people lead you to where they are in their grief.

10. Provide student/family with information about community resources if needed.

Depending on your community, the effect violence in our nation has had on your schools, and the extent to which you want to cover a broad base of possible crisis events that could occur, other areas covered in the crisis manual might include intruders in buildings, hostage situations, bomb threats, building evacuation/alternative school locations, chemical spill/toxic fumes, and suicide threats. An advantage to including these and other topics in the manual may insure that if staff have all crisis procedures in one manual, they may use the manual.

An Intruder in the Building

Recently a patron was wandering around in a school and a teacher approached him inquiring if he needed assistance. He replied that he did not and the teacher said, "OK, have a nice day." Most schools in America have signs on their doors indicating that "visitors should report to the office." Let's get real! How many times do you think that an individual or group of individuals who want to disrupt the school day or harm to staff or students are going to report to the office prior to completing their intended mission?

Given that all school districts, no matter their size, may have intruder problems, the following are some examples of information that should appear in the crisis manual.

1. The first person to notice an intruder (person with a weapon or person who is upset or acting out of control) will notify the principal.

2. The principal or a representative will sound a planned alarm. For example:

   a. In a building with an intercom system, "Mr. Green is in the building."

   b. Other buildings could use a long bell ring, i.e., 10 seconds.

3. Alarm sounded means: Lock your classroom door, do not allow your students to leave the classroom; be seated on the floor next to an interior wall away from windows and doors until further notice.

4. Teachers take an accurate count of students.

5. The staff communicates to the office any information regarding the intruder.

6. The principal will determine the need to notify the police and the school superintendent of any emergency situation.

Hostage Situation

May 16, 1986, Cokeville, a small rural Wyoming community, was one of the first school districts in the nation to experience a highly publicized hostage/bombing situation. A man and woman entered the school with a homemade bomb and took some students and staff hostage. The end result was that the bomb exploded, injuring about 80 people. If it can happen in Cokeville, it can and does happen elsewhere. Even though the odds may be a hostage situation will never occur in your schools, forewarned is forearmed. Keep the following suggestions in mind as you prepare this section of your crisis manual.

1. Call 911.

2. Do not do anything to escalate the situation before law enforcement arrives. (In rural settings, law enforcement response may be delayed in arriving, so you may need to design some contingency plans.)

3. Notify the superintendent's office.

4. Designate personnel to monitor hallways and other areas of the building and to direct students not in class to a safe area.

5. Assign a staff member to liaison with law enforcement authorities.

6. Inform the office staff as to appropriate information to give callers. (If your patrons have law enforcement frequency scanners, they will be curious to say the least.)

7. The principal or a representative will sound a planned alarm similar to that used for an intruder, for example:

   a. In buildings with an intercom system: "Mrs. White is in the building."

   b. Other buildings could use a designated bell ring.

8. Teachers should not allow students to leave the classroom and should direct them to be seated on the floor next to an interior wall away from windows and doors. Students should only be allowed to leave the classroom when the all-clear announcement is given or when directed to move to another location by administrators or law enforcement authorities.

9. Make a list of those being held hostage.

10. Keep the media informed of the situation so parents will have accurate information.

11. Plan how to inform families of students and staff directly affected.

12. Contact the crisis team to assist students and staff in dealing with the aftermath. (If you move students to alternative school sites, you may want crisis team members at those sites to work with the students and staff.)

Chemical Spills/Toxic Fumes

A school district in a western state had asked a committee to develop a general crisis plan. During the committee's lunch break, a truck carrying a toxic gas was involved in an accident just down the street from where the committee was working on the plan. When the committee members returned from lunch, they found they were unable to continue their work because the authorities had evacuated the area. When the committee was finally given permission to return to their work, they immediately decided that a section on chemical spills and toxic fumes should be a part of a general crisis response plan.

Many schools have effective plans already established for accidental chemical spills that may occur in the school building. Suggestions for chemical spill or toxic fumes that may occur outside the school building include:

1. Keep students inside.

2. Close the windows.

3. Don't go near or step in spilled material.

4. Establish contact with law enforcement, fire, and health officials.

5. Establish contact with the superintendent's office.

6. Be prepared to evacuate the building. (Schools should plan where they would take students in the event they would need to evacuate the school building. Keep in mind sending students outdoors may not be possible at certain times of the year. If students are outside, move them upwind.

Bomb Threat Procedures

Places as small as the school in Cokeville and as big as the World Trade Center can be targets for bombs. Because this risk is ever present, it is incumbent on school officials to have a general plan of procedure for handling the threat of a bombing. Although not always the case, the psyche of a bomber is such that he or she frequently calls to warn of the impending doom or the threat of it. Suggested procedures include:

1. Upon receipt of a bomb threat, the person receiving the call will make every attempt to:

    a. Prolong the conversation. ***Do not hang up the phone.*** (Use another phone to call authorities.)

    b. Identify background noises and any distinguishing voice characteristics.

    c. Ask the caller for a description of the bomb, where it is, and when it is due to explode.

2. The person receiving the threat will notify the principal immediately.

3. Alert 911.

4. The principal will, in consulting with authorities, decide whether to make a preliminary search or to evacuate the building.

5. Notify the superintendent's office.

6. Inform staff and students of the bomb threat and also give any immediate directions, for example, remain in their rooms until an all-clear is given or directions to evacuate.

7. Ask staff to make a visual observation of their classroom/work area and inform them not to open cabinets, doors or move objects. If anything suspicious is found, **Do not touch it!** The bomb can be almost anything from a bundle of dynamite to concealed or ordinary objects (briefcase, toolbox, or pieces of pipe). You will be searching for something that doesn't belong in the classroom/work area.

8. Check the absentee list and on each absentee from class at the time the threat was received. Account for all students, check halls and rest rooms.

9. Ask for volunteers to participate in the search with law enforcement/fire department.

10. Meet with law enforcement/fire department and search team to decide on the procedure for checking the building.

11. If at any time the threat is determined to be valid, use standard fire drill procedures with any necessary modifications to evacuate the building. Evacuate at least 300 feet from the building. Plan for an alternate location if needed due to a prolonged search or inclement weather.

12. When the building is reported to be safe, resume whatever schedule is needed for the rest of the day and debrief staff and students.

13. If a written threat is received, copy the contents and protect the original message (plastic or other covering) to preserve fingerprints and other identifying marks.

14. Use the Bomb Threat Checklist to gather helpful information. (See Appendix A, page 204.)

After Thoughts

School crisis response plans are a dime a dozen in the 2000s. The majority of school districts have seen the need, or felt the pressure, to formulate in writing the general procedures that should be adhered to in the event of a school emergency or tragedy and the resulting crisis that potentially could impact significant numbers of students and staff. Schools have developed, bought, borrowed, or downloaded these plans and have shared the plans with staff and, in some

cases, students and the community. General planning for a school crisis usually involves determining all of the possible crisis events with potential to impact a school and disrupt learning, putting together a booklet, pamphlet, or something in a printed format outlining predetermined procedures for perceived school crisis events, and distributing copies of a pre-designed plan to all interested parties. It also usually involves tabletop sessions on various crises scenarios and the schools' and emergency responders' response to the perceived event. General planning usually includes providing staff development concerning what may be expected of them during a school crisis event and instruction on procedures and protocols for staff to follow. Planning for a school crisis also *may* involve drills and practice responding to a school crisis.

For years, and by law, schools have practiced fire drills and sometimes weather-related or natural disaster drills. As important as these drills are, too often they are met with complacency and apathy. When schools practice any drills, they should consider practicing responses to an unnatural or unplanned occurrence that may happen in the event of a real fire or event prompting the evacuation of the school. (See Chapter 16 for information on handling unplanned events during a school emergency.)

In addition to fire and natural disaster drills, some schools practice intruder and other types of terrorism drills. Although all emergency drills may have some protocols in common, intruder and other terrorist drills may preclude the need to seek safety in the school building as opposed to leaving the building. The school's general crisis response plan should outline procedures for "hold in place" drills including:

- Specific codes notifying staff to stay in their assigned areas. School districts should consider using the same coding for all buildings in the district.

- Locking classroom doors. Many classroom doors lock from the outside thus requiring school personnel to step into the hallway to secure classroom doors.

- Procedures for dealing with students who are in the school hallways or restrooms. Although staff may be encouraged to "retrieve" students from hallways, restrooms, or other areas of the school to get those students into more safe areas, some staff may be reluctant to move into what may potentially be harm's way.

- Dealing with students who do not want to remain in a potentially secure area during a school emergency. Schools often do a good job of training staff in lockdown procedures, but fail to properly train staff in dealing with students who are anxious about being contained in the school, especially when they may hear shots or explosions or perceive it would be in their best interest to leave the lock down area.

- Schools without intercoms must have effective and consistent means to notify staff of potentially dangerous situations that may require containing students in safe areas. Schools with general plans or plans "borrowed" from other school districts may not accommodate the facilities disparity between schools.

The general school plan should be reviewed on an annual basis. At or near the beginning of each school year, the school district's crisis response team(s), the school district's administrative team, and other interested parties should meet to review the district's general crisis response plan. Not only is this annual meeting important, it is imperative that all parties responsible for crisis response be "at the table." This meeting is another opportunity to ensure that students and staff members will receive timely and appropriate response during a crisis impacting the school.

Based on an annual plan review, some alternations may be made in the school district's general crisis response plan. Plan changes impacting staff should be immediately communicated, and in the event of significant changes in the plan, staff may need additional crisis training.

At the beginning of each school year, all new staff should receive a copy of the school district's crisis response plan. In some instances, these plans can be voluminous and cumbersome. Although staff may be required to keep their plan in a prominent place at their work site, it should be noted that if the school's crisis plan is lengthy, staff may have difficulty locating appropriate sections of the plan during a school emergency. To offset this possibility, school districts may want to consider a one- or two-page set of specific directions covering most probable school crisis events to supplement the basic general plan. This brief set of emergency instructions should be in a large font, enabling staff to easily discern information during stressful and frightening crisis events.

Chapter 3

The Media

A Funky Winkerbean cartoon begins with a television talk show host commenting to a principal, "As a high school principal, have you ever done a talk show before, Fred?" "No," the principal replied. "Well," continued the talk show host, "Just relax and we'll do everything we can to make it a comfortable and fun experience for you." The director of the show signals for it to begin, the red light on the TV camera blinks on, and the talk show host says, "We're facing a CRISIS in education in this country, and with me today is one of the people personally responsible...."

America's educational system has often been the whipping post of this country's powerful and influential media. Although the influence of the media can be substantial, with preparation and training we can learn skills to assist us in successfully working with the media. And at no other time may this be more important than during a time of school crisis when emotions may be running high and it seems like almost everything is beyond our control. It is during these times school staff's media skills can be put to the supreme test.

What do we know about the media? We know there are basically three types of media: print (newspapers, magazines), audio (radio), and audio visual (television). All have their unique market in the communication industry. All may come knocking on your door at any time. All have a job to provide their consumers with the most up to date and accurate information possible. All deserve and should receive our cooperation.

What else do we know about the media? We know they may not use all of the information we share and may take things out of context. We know they can put a "spin" on a story to catch the public's attention and that may alter the consumers perception as to what may actually be occurring. We know at times they may seem to infringe on people's "space." We know the "power of the pen" is mighty and you should not get in an ink throwing contest with someone who buys ink by the barrel. We know some people like to read about themselves, hear themselves, or see themselves, even though they may not be the best resources for accurate and complete information.

We also know the first amendment to the Constitution of the United States of America guarantees the right of free speech to all people across this land. Therefore, school district staff need to acquire and refine the media skills necessary to prepare for the good times as well as the bad.

The Media Contact Person

As reflected in the General Plan, the superintendent should be notified immediately when the media has contacted a school and is seeking information or an interview. In some school districts the superintendent is the designated spokesperson for the media and all media contact is coordinated through that office. Larger school districts may have an information specialist who coordinates all media contacts.

A Midwestern school superintendent required all media contacts go through him. On the day a senior girl hung herself in the shower of the school's locker room, the superintendent was attending an out of state conference. The high school principal was attending the conference with the superintendent and the school district's assistant superintendent was in the state capitol at a legislative hearing.

Try to imagine the confusion and panic that occurred during this school crisis. The end result was the school crisis team not only had to manage the crisis at hand, but they also were confronted with another crisis, managing the media.

Caution should be exercised in designing a media plan that is people specific. For example, if the school district's crisis response plan designates the superintendent of schools as the only media spokesperson, this would require that the superintendent should be available at all times. In reality, as the chief spokesperson for the school district, the superintendent may be required to represent the district at various meetings and conventions both state and nationwide. If possible, details regarding "chain of command" should be worked out prior to any event that may draw the attention of the media. The crisis response plan should identify those staff who have been trained in working with the media. If necessary, an "on call" list should be established to insure the availability of a media spokesperson.

Given all the issues that may arise during times of crisis, school administrators may not even be the appropriate persons to be school district spokespersons for the media. Let's assume a school district administrator, being interviewed by a television correspondent, gives information in error. The error could have occurred because the administrator was misinformed, misstated, misled, missed a briefing meeting, misunderstood, or just plain made a mistake. If at all possible, district administrators should avoid being placed in positions that may affect their leadership role with the public. An administrator who has miscommunicated with the public during times of crisis may not be able to gain the confidence of the public during budget hearings, school referendums, and other situations.

If not a district administrator or an information specialist, who should serve as the media representative? Consideration should be given to having a member of the crisis response team serve as the school district's spokesperson for the media. Look at the advantages.

Crisis response team members are involved in the response from the beginning. They have up to date knowledge of the details and are aware of the various issues concerning the event. They have been talking with students, staff, and parents throughout the event and have a feel for the tempo of the situation. They have been involved in all of the planning and update meetings and probably have not been distracted by other concerns, i.e., meetings on issues other than the crisis event, distractions due to previous commitments and scheduled appointments, and unplanned situations which arise that have nothing to do with the crisis event but require an administrator's attention. Additionally, administrators may have some difficulty working with the media in that they need to maintain media relationships. Whereas, the crisis response team person does not have to work with the media on a regular basis.

If a crisis response team person makes a mistake in an interview, which seldom happens, a district administrator, i.e., superintendent, assistant superintendent, or principal can correct the information, if necessary. It appears that this is a win-win situation for the school district. They have a well practiced and competent crisis response team spokesperson who most likely will handle the situation extremely well. Additionally, they have a district administrator who can focus on other details of work, yet correct or expand, if necessary, on media issues concerning the crisis event.

A northwest United States school district decided to hold tryouts for the position of media spokesperson in times of crisis. Applicants ranged from district administrators to members of the classified staff. The plan called for a local television reporter to interview prospective candidates at a television studio. The school district's crisis response team was asked to develop a scenario that would set the stage for the interviews.

The crisis team wrote a scenario entitled, "The Case of the Tainted Tacos." The situation was tacos were served for lunch in the school cafeteria and some students got a minor case of food poisoning and had to go home.

The first person to be interviewed by the television reporter was the school district's purchasing agent. The Purchasing agent had been given a copy of the scenario five minutes prior to the scheduled interview.

The television studio lights rose to full power and the camera began running as the reporter, noted for his tough interviews, asked, "Can you tell me what happened?" The Purchasing agent replied, "We have a case of food poisoning." The reporter retorted, "Are you a licensed physician?" The purchasing agent, beginning to squirm, replied, "I have talked to the vendor who sold us the tacos and they have guaranteed they will replace them!" Snickers progressed to laughter. Even the purchasing agent, once he realized what he had said, joined in. Needless to say, the individual was not selected as the district's media spokesperson for crisis events. The "winner" that evening was a crisis team member who, half way through the interview with the reporter announced, "This interview has to stop right now! I had lunch at school today and I'm not feeling very well!"

No matter who the school district selects for their media spokesperson in times of tragedy, it is important that the individual:

a. Be verbally adroit or skillful.

b. Be calm under pressure.

c. Be a quick thinker.

d. Have the skill to turn a potential media disaster into a positive situation.

e. Be available when tragedy strikes.

f. Be willing to practice and upgrade media skills.

Tips for Interviews

No matter which media (print, radio, television) you are working with, there are a set of generally agreed guidelines that should be followed.

1. Be honest. If you don't know the answer, say so. Tell reporters you will get back to them with the answers as soon as you can. If you make a mistake in an interview, say so.

2. There is no such thing as "off the record."

3. If you are in a room with a microphone or television cameras, always assume they are on.

4. Try to have a goal for the interview. What do you want to accomplish?

5. Prepare for your interview. If you need more time, ask for it.

6. Understand what you are going to say so that you talk about the topic knowledgeably.

7. Anticipate the "worst question" you may have to answer and plan for that in advance.

8. Bridge a question from where you are in the interview to where you want to be. Different information may be related in some manner.

9. Never say, "no comment." It makes you sound like you have something to hide.

10. Don't use jargon. You won't have a translator.

Preparation for Interviews

When grief visits school, it may, and often does, seem like there is little time to work on other issues. All of the staff are busy with the task at hand as well as performing their respective duties. Then along comes a request to meet with some contingent of the media. The temptation may be to "wing it" with the media and get back to the task at hand—the crisis.

Preparation for media interviews is important. So important that many crisis teams have specific plans in place to allow for consultation and preparation. During this time of preparation be sure to:

A. Assess your audience. What audience is the reporter representing? Ask how the interview is to be used. If it is for a newscast, very short, 10- to 30-second cuts may be used. If it's for a longer talk show, the whole conversation may be used.

B. Ask in advance of the interview what questions will be asked so you have a chance to prepare to give complete information. Ask, "What kinds of things about the topic would you like to know so I can give you specific information? You may be surprised at how willing the media is to cooperate with you in getting the most complete and accurate story possible. Remember, they have a job to do and they want to do it as completely and professionally as possible.

Newspaper/Magazine Interviews

It can happen to anyone. An interview is granted, a story is written and published. You are dismayed that what you thought you said and what comes out in print are not the same. Don't be too quick to blame the reporter. The fault may be yours.

Most print media reporters rely on the notes they take during an interview to guide them in the creation of their story. Unlike radio and television, your comments are usually not recorded. That situation alone means you will need to prepare differently for your interview with a tabloid reporter.

Some suggestions for interviewing with the press are:

A. Provide supplemental materials in writing to assist the reporter in better understanding the story being covered.

B. Use an outline to keep you focused on the main points you wish to cover in the interview.

C. Do not write the story for the reporter. You may want to provide the reporter with your outline instead of giving a prepared statement.

D. Ask the reporter to give general feedback on parts of the interview that may be confusing or you are concerned may have been misunderstood. If necessary, reframe the reporter's version of what you have said.

E. When the interview is completed, offer to be receptive to any follow up questions the reporter may have when writing the story.

F. Don't hesitate to ask the reporter if you can read the story before going to press. If this is allowed, you get one more chance to make certain that the story is an accurate reflection of the interview.

Radio Interviews

During times of crisis, remember the phones in your school are both a source of receiving information and giving information. More than one school district has received a call from a radio station wanting information about the crisis event and how it is being handled only to find out later the school secretary responded to the questions and thus became their media spokesperson for the school district. This is all right if the secretary is the designated spokesperson and has the information and training to do the interview. Unfortunately, there maybe sometimes that is not the case.

Some suggestions for interviewing with the radio media are:

A. Beware of background noises, no matter if the interview is being conducted over the phone or in person.

B. Don't use the reporter's name in the answer to try to personalize the interview unless the whole conversation will be used. It makes it awkward for another announcer to use the tape cut later.

C. Respond in complete sentences. Mention the topic in the answer. ("We are working with students who are grieving the death of John Doe.")

D. Leave short pauses to make it easier for the reporter to edit your comments. Don't interrupt the end of a question. (They will edit the tape, so make their job as easy as possible.)

E. Put energy in your voice. Don't read a statement; it may sound like it is being read. Instead, write down a list of important ideas and fill in the exact wording as you go through the interview.

Television Interviews

Lights! Camera! Action! Words that would increase almost anyone's heart rate. Even television veterans admit to an occasional adrenaline rush. Television is perhaps the most difficult of all the media interviews and the most effective. Not only does the public have an opportunity to hear how the school district is successfully managing the crisis but, they can visually see the calming presence the media spokesperson is projecting. It is the ultimate in communication and, as suggested earlier, it can be a powerful part of the crisis response arsenal.

Some suggestions for interviewing with the television media are:

A. Remember, television is a two-dimensional medium. How you sit or stand is important. Sit back in your chair, leaning slightly forward during the interview. If standing, stand still. Rocking back and forth projects a sign of nervousness.

B. Dress for success. Do not wear small, even patterns. They tend to make your face appear to be the brightest spot on the television screen. Dark blue colors frequently look more intense on the camera. The best colors to wear are light blues, pink, lavender or tan.

C. Be aware of the background. Know what you are standing or sitting in front of and avoid distracting objects in the background. (One school district always did their television interviews in front of the flag pole on the school ground. Persons being interviewed usually looked like they had this long pole growing out of their heads.) Brick walls are not a good background either.

D. If the reporter is standing to the side of the camera, decide whether you are going to look at the camera or the reporter. Looking from one to the other is distracting to the viewer and presents a nervous appearance.

E. When you have completed your response to a question, wait for another question from the reporter. If the reporter does not ask a question immediately, just wait. All too often the person being interviewed becomes uncomfortable with the silence and begins to talk randomly. Sometimes that leads to trouble. Keep quiet and wait for the next question.

F. Upon completion of the interview, the reporter (this is true of all forms of the media) may ask you if you have forgotten anything or if there is anything you wish to add. If you have completed your goal for the interview, decline the opportunity and conclude the interview. If the reporter did not ask you "the worst question," consider yourself lucky and get back to the crisis at hand.

The Rest of the Story

No matter which branch of the media you are working with, *Do not allow them into the school where the crisis is occurring.* You have an obligation to protect the privacy of your students and staff. The First Amendment says there is a right to free speech. It does not say that reporters can come onto school grounds and into school buildings to get their stories. However, if you do not cooperate and grant an interview, reporters may interview students or staff off campus, i.e., homes, fast food establishments, and student hangouts. Give the media the story they have a right and a duty to report and remember your obligations to your students and staff in doing so.

After Thoughts

Dealing successfully with the media is key if the outcome of a crisis event is to be positive. Schools should be prepared to respond to media requests for information as quickly as is practical during or after a crisis event. Press conferences, depending on the number of media inquiries, may be the most efficient and effective way of working with representatives of the media. Although a press conference may be efficient, the actual press conference may be intimidating.

Do not be afraid of the media. View media as an opportunity to communicate with students and staff across the school district as well as with parents and patrons. In the event of a school evacuation and possible confusion during the early stages of a school emergency, the media can actually be helpful in getting factual information to the people who need it.

A press conference should be held away from the site of the school crisis. Depending on the crisis event, school officials may experience people other than the media attending the conference. Law enforcement and other emergency response personnel, as well as elected officials, may want to speak to the media as well. It is imperative coordination exist between the different entities participating in the conference. More than one school district has been embarrassed in a press conference when information was revealed which the school considered not in the best interests of students and staff. Depending on the crisis event, press conferences have the potential to become raucous, with questions being fired at the conference presenters. A circus atmosphere is not what schools need or want.

School districts, *prior* to a crisis event, should meet with media spokespersons from emergency response agencies to discuss media relations during emergency events. As much as possible, roles of all interested parties should be established and strategies for successful media conferences should be explored.

A significant media issue for schools can be the hyping in the media of previous school crisis events at the time of the anniversary of the event. One need only watch yearly revisits to national crisis events to get a taste of the media's appetite for revisiting tragic events on at least an annual basis. The media may even desire to interview individuals or groups who were most impacted when the tragedy occurred. When this happens, schools may be caught between trying to protect privacy, which might be in the best interest of some students, and being accused of stonewalling and being uncooperative.

To assist in helping schools deal with media coverage of crisis events, school officials and school media spokespersons should hold annual meetings with media assigned to cover school events. Establishing positive working relationships with media is important, no matter if the school has a crisis event or not.

One of the problems in working with some media sources is the turnover among media field reporters at the local level. Another problem is that field reporters are sometimes instructed by their superiors to be more aggressive and dramatic in reporting crisis events, past or present. Meeting with media during less stressful times may help ameliorate certain types of media reporting. Keep in mind that the media will not contact the school to set up such meetings, so school personnel need to be proactive and persistent to insure such meetings take place.

As our nation experiences threats and actions that either directly impact students and staff or, at the very least, frighten them, national and local media will continue to be interested in the school's reaction to the events and the impact those events may have on student learning. More and more schools have developed opportunities and materials for talking to students about war, terrorism, and disaster. Sharing these materials with media and enlisting their aid in raising community awareness to the needs of its citizens, of all ages, is yet another way to establish good working relationships.

During local, national, or international crisis events, some staff in schools may determine that students should be exposed to media coverage of those events. Some school staff members may even rationalize that those events are "history in the making" and students should be a part of the experience. Prior to such times, school administrators should work with staff members in developing clear objectives and parameters for student exposure to events commanding media coverage. Some possible student exposure to media guidelines should include:

- Students should not be exposed to violent and graphic events.

- Students should be able to have alternate curriculum experiences other than reading about, listening to, or viewing the media coverage of a tragic or frightening event.

- Parents should be informed their students may be exposed to certain media coverage, and parents' wishes regarding the amount or lack of media exposure they desire for their children should be respected.

- School crisis team members should be activated if there is a possibility exposure to certain media coverage may create student fear and anxiety.

- Alternate ways of keeping students and staff abreast of some national or international crisis events, other than direct media exposure, should be explored. (Some school districts provide periodic daily updates to staff via e-mail or written statements with suggestions and guidelines on sharing the information with their students.)

Chapter 4

The Specific Plan

The general plan is designed to provide broad guidelines for a crisis response and outline a sense of direction for various tragedies. The specific plan is written after the crisis has occurred and is designed to provide details as to how the event is to be managed. To illustrate the specific plan, let's deal with an actual crisis.

Your team receives a call at 4:00 in the afternoon. The information details a motorcycle/school bus accident. A senior in your high school and his girl friend, also a senior, are riding on a motorcycle in a residential area near an elementary school. A school bus, occupied by 27 elementary students, makes a left turn just as the motorcycle crests a hill. Unable to stop, the motorcycle collides with the right front portion of the school bus.

The school bus brakes. After the school bus comes to a halt, the driver stands up and yells at the students, "This never would have happened if you had been sitting in your seats."

The driver of the motorcycle is killed instantly and his girl-friend is critically injured. A complicating factor is one of the elementary students on the school bus is the sister of the girl who was on the back of the motorcycle.

Obviously, it would be impossible to design a plan in advance covering the various situations that present themselves. The general plan would provide the team with guidelines on procedures—all the way from contacting the crisis team, notifying school district administrators, activating the calling tree to notify certified and classified staff, to the funeral and the "lingering death" (she did survive) of the high school girl and everything in between. A specific plan dealing with the motorcycle/school bus crisis event might proceed in this manner.

Verify

Immediately, using as many reliable sources as possible, verify the crisis event information. What are reliable sources? Usually law enforcement, hospitals, and certain county or state officials are sources of reliable information. Sometimes school staff, students, parents, and the media also are reliable sources of information. A good example of misinformation is obvious in this example.

An office staff person in a high school received a call inform-ing the school that "John Doe" would not be in school that day because he had committed suicide the night before. The office staff person, wanting to make sure that all students and staff immediately knew what had happened, drafted an announce-ment concerning the death of the student and quickly had it circulated to all of the high school classrooms.

As one of the staff members was reading the announcement to the class, she happened to glance over the top of the piece of paper she was reading and, to her surprise, there sat the student who was to have killed himself. This was an embarrassing situation.

No matter what the source, check the information as thoroughly as possible and know what was once reliable information may change. To illustrate this point, a young student running across the street was struck by a car and killed. Shortly after the accident, law enforcement officials informed the school's crisis response team the student was legally in the crosswalk and had a green light. Several hours after the accident, when the law enforcement officials concluded interviewing several witnesses, it was determined the student had crossed the street on a red light. When attempting to verify information seek the most reliable information possible and realize the story may change as new information is revealed.

Notifying District Administrators

Always notify district administrators when tragedy strikes your school district. It is essential the school superintendent and his or her administrative team be aware of what is happening and be given the latest and most accurate information concerning the event. This is true whether the administrators are in or out of the community at the time of the crisis.

It should not be the role of the crisis team, however, to inform the school district's board of education. Superintendents or their designates perform this task.

Calling Tree

A district administrator, preferably the building principal, should be responsible to activate a calling tree. The calling tree is a listing of all certified and classified staff who are connected with the school. In the case of the motorcycle/school bus accident, this would probably include the high school staff and the staff from the sixth grade sister's elementary school.

The calling tree remains in operation until all staff have been notified of the crisis and have received information, i.e., the time of special staff meetings and basic details regarding the crisis. If the communication breaks down along the way or the calling tree becomes a "gossip tree," some staff will not have the information needed to make some decisions for themselves, their fellow staff, and their families.

Sometimes schools develop last minute calling trees during a time of crisis. This can add to the confusion and may heighten the anxiety of staff if they are not accustomed to this method of receiving information. Plant your calling tree now. If it hasn't been tended (used) for a while, nurture it and see if it still bears fruit. (Try it and see if it still works.)

Notifying the Crisis Response Team

Just as a school needs a plan for notifying staff, crisis teams need a plan to notify team members. Simple as it may sound, contacting crisis response team members can be a problem unless there is a specific procedure for contacting them.

Crisis teams usually consist of five to six members, one of whom is the team leader. In most instances it is the team leader's responsibility to contact the team members during times of tragedy. A list of home and work numbers is usually sufficient.

The design of a plan for team contact needs to take into account the fact people are not always at home or at work. They can be out of town, gone for the evening, or on an extended vacation. Therefore, it is incumbent on individual team members to let the team leader know if they will be away for any extended period of time or where the alternate (substitute) can be reached.

Some crisis response teams assign alternates to cover for a team member who is out of town, ill, or unable to respond due to extenuating circumstances. This enables the team leader to be certain there will be enough team members available to respond to the crisis.

Technology has also enhanced the ability of team leaders to contact their teams. Electronic pagers and cellular telephones provide more flexibility for crisis response teams and assure school officials these teams can be contacted day or night. Some schools have been successful in obtaining communication equipment from local businesses at reduced rates or at no cost.

Some school districts are assisted in this effort through help from local service clubs.

Crisis Team Meeting

The crisis team leader, when contacting the crisis team, should arrange for a meeting of team members. This meeting is an opportunity for the team members to put together a specific plan for managing the crisis event. At this early stage, this is a tentative plan. The plan becomes the "official plan" after it is reviewed and approved by the administrative team. One of the keys to success in crisis management is the design of this plan by the team. The tentative plan *should not* be written at a combined meeting of administrators and crisis team members. It should be written by the crisis team and presented to the administrative team for approval.

Meeting with Administrators

If possible, a meeting should be planned with those building and district administrators who are affected by the event. At this meeting the specific plan, based on the crisis team's training, experience, expertise, and assessment of the situation at hand, is outlined by the crisis team leader with support from the team. Given the motorcycle/ school bus scenario, the proposed plan would cover every aspect of the response including meetings with students, staff, and parents; setting up a crisis room in the high school; writing an announcement for students and staff and a letter for parents; following the dead student's class schedule; dealing with the dead student's possessions; appropriate responses to requests for memorials; managing the situation with the hospitalized girl and helping her sister and family; and working with the dead student's family regarding some of the details of the funeral.

Administrators attending the meeting will review each phase of the proposed plan. Necessary adjustments should be made and mutually agreed upon. The end result would be a specific plan for the upcoming day(s) with "just in case" options built into the plan.

The Morning Staff Meeting

The morning staff meeting (See Chapter 6) is an opportunity to meet with certified and classified staff and outline the strategy for the day. Some school districts even design their general response plans based on having a morning staff meeting.

However, some school crisis teams become so focused on the morning staff meeting that when an event occurs during the day, they have difficulty with their response. Be certain that your crisis response teams practice scenarios that require responding without a morning staff meeting.

The morning staff meeting needs to be held as early in the school day as possible to give staff sufficient time to organize themselves before students begin arriving at school. A common complaint from teaching staff is the morning staff meeting is not concluded before students began to arrive for the school day. Staff need time to collect their thoughts and be physically and emotionally prepared before the students arrive.

It is imperative, if at all possible, for the building administrator to be in charge of the morning staff meeting. The administrator's presence usually has a calming effect on staff and assures everyone everything is under control. If a "stranger" conducts the meeting, staff anxiety may be heightened.

The physical setting for the meeting is important. All staff should be seated and the acoustics should be such that everyone in the room can hear without straining. Comments like, "We can't hear the questions being asked," usually make people more anxious. They may be thinking, "If they can't even organize this meeting, how can they organize the response for the entire day?"

The morning staff meeting provides opportunities other than just giving the staff information. It is an opportunity to rally staff support for each other and "eyeball" staff to see how they are doing. Done properly, this meeting may give clues as to which staff members may be having difficulty handling the situation. Keep in mind some staff may require assistance, either because the crisis event is bothering them or the current situation has triggered memories from previous events in their lives. Either way, plans should have been made to assist these individuals. Substitutes should have been called ahead of time just in case one or more of the staff members are unable to report for their duties.

If at all possible, the morning staff meeting should conclude on a positive note. Staff should leave feeling confident about the plan for the day ahead and assured competent help is available should they need it.

The Announcement

The announcement (See Chapter 5) should be written by the crisis response team and presented to the administrative team for their approval. If there is a before school staff meeting, the announcement should be distributed to staff with directions as to when it shall be read to the students in their classrooms. In the case of the motorcycle/bus accident, the appropriate plan would be to read the announcement to the high school students shortly after attendance is taken. The announcement should be read to all students. There have been situations where the announcement was not read to all students under the assumption some students were already aware of the crisis. Crisis teams or school's staff should not speculate as to which students may or may not be aware of the crisis situation. It may be necessary, however, to identify close friends of the student who has died or been injured and give them the opportunity to learn of the crisis in a more private setting, i.e., individually or in a small group. Under no circumstances would this announcement be read to students in groups larger than classroom size. Some schools have moved entire student bodies into the auditorium or gymnasium for the purpose of informing all students at the same time. This technique may result in a larger number of students being affected by the crisis event than would have been affected if the students had been informed in a classroom setting.

The Letter

The common vehicle used to give students information about the crisis situation is the all school announcement. To inform parents, a letter (See Chapter 12) should be sent home with students or mailed to parents giving each family information on what has occurred and what the school district is doing to assist their student(s). This letter, written by the crisis team and edited and signed by the building principal, has proved to be an important crisis response tool in communicating and working with parents.

Crisis Rooms

Students and staff need a place to express and share their grief during times of tragedy. One of the features of the specific plan is setting up rooms for students and staff who are unable to be in their classrooms.

The student crisis room (See Chapter 9) can be anywhere in the school building. Preferably it is a room large enough to accommodate all of the students who need a place to grieve. If possible, it should be a room that can be used throughout the day and will not require students to be moved to another room for any reason. Schools report when they move students from one designated crisis room to another, it is confusing, embarrassing to some students, and other students tend to "join up" with the students in the crisis room. As one staff member put it, "When students changing crisis rooms meet the students in the hall who are headed to algebra, sometimes the students going to algebra join up with the grieving students instead of going to algebra to grieve algebra."

If possible, avoid using media centers, administrative centers, commons areas, student lounges, or other high traffic areas of the building as crisis rooms. When these areas are used for crisis rooms, there is a tendency to disrupt routine activities for students. Keep in mind it is unusual for all students to be affected by the crisis event. Given the opportunity, many students will want and need the instructional routine of the school day. Caution should also be exercised in using the counseling center as a crisis room for students. A mid-Atlantic states counselor recalled a high school student who came into the counseling center only to see all of the counseling staff involved in working with grieving students. The student became hysterical and threw an unoccupied chairs against the wall. One of the counselors, hearing the commotion, escorted the student into one of the counseling offices and closed the door. The counselor knew the student and commented he was surprised the student was a close friend of the students involved in the accident. "I hardly knew them," replied the student, "but the only way to get in to see a counselor without waiting is to create a disturbance. I need a letter of recommendation from my counselor for a college application that needs to be in the mail today and I'm afraid that I'll miss the afternoon mail."

Instructions should be given to staff that they should not send more than two students at a time from their classroom to the crisis room. Using these guidelines, the flow of students in and out of the crisis room is more orderly and manageable. However, some staff may send several students at a time to the crisis room. As one staff member was overheard saying in the classroom, "If you people are going to cry and carry on like that, why don't you all go down to that room where the criers are." Remember that emotions can run very high particularly in the early stages of a crisis response. Be prepared for the unexpected. Twenty-seven students descending on a crisis center, all from one class, may fit the category of "the unexpected."

It's not uncommon for staff to be concerned some students are taking advantage of the crisis situation and are just hanging out in the crisis room instead of attending classes. In some instances, that may be an accurate assessment. Therefore, in some middle and high school settings, it is advisable to encourage students, particularly at the end of each instructional period, to see if they can return to their classes. Students may appreciate the chance to move back into their routine. Some students are in the crisis room, not because they knew the students who were killed or injured, but because the event has triggered something else that is causing them difficulty. Give them the opportunity to share their concerns.

School staff should also have a place where they can share their grief about the current situation or other hurts in their lives that the event may have triggered. This room should not be the faculty study/lounge, but it should be a separate room. Although a small percent of the staff may take advantage of this opportunity, it is well worth the effort.

Crisis rooms are usually staffed by a couple of members of the crisis response team. At times there may be building staff assisting in the rooms.

Using Mental Health Staff/Clergy for Crisis Response

There is some debate and at times much discussion as to the practice of bringing in outsiders to assist schools during times of crisis. There are school districts that use outsiders as their primary means of responding to tragedy. Their logic is these people have more experience in dealing with crisis issues and have the training required to successfully handle crisis situations. Privately, some school administrators confess they do not want the responsibility of dealing with major crisis situations and it is easier to hand them over to professionals from outside the school.

In school districts where accessibility to mental health staff is limited, schools have asked members of the clergy to come into the school to assist with the crisis response. Sometimes all clergy in the community are asked to help, but more frequently, it is the clergy that either volunteer their services or clergy who may be more familiar to school staff, i.e., from churches staff members attend.

Again, this method of responding to school tragedies may at times have some successes, but the probability for creating an additional crisis should be kept in mind. Schools using or considering the use of this response option need to assess the potential risks as well as the benefits.

Most people in our country have a common frame of reference. They went to school. Granted, their length of time in school and their experiences may vary widely. This is especially true for mental health professionals and members of the clergy who most likely have had to spend large amounts of time in instructional settings. It should be remembered, however, there is a difference between having been in a school setting at one time and working in the schools of the Nineties. Just because people went to school some years ago does not mean they are familiar with the schools of today. When school district staff contact mental health professionals to come into the schools, they frequently contact "certain" people. This might be a mental health agency or specific individuals. Mental health professionals who are less familiar to school staff may not be contacted to assist. This practice creates the potential for conflict of interest or, at best, displeased mental health professionals. These people may feel the need to contact board members or school officials to express their displeasure. Sometimes their attorneys do it for them!

"Mr. _____ , I don't have the time to help your student today, but if you would like to make an appointment to send him to my office, I think I can be of help. Of course, you will have to pay my hourly fee."

This was a conversation overheard on a school telephone between a mental health professional brought in to help a school during a crisis and a parent of a student. It goes without saying, use caution in allowing private enterprise access to students in a school setting.

Similar issues may arise when clergy come into school settings to work with students. Having a Catholic priest counseling a Methodist student, or whatever the combination, may cause more problems than it solves. Encouraging students and parents to seek assistance through the churches of their choice may be more prudent than bringing clergy into the schools. For private and parochial schools, the option is quite different. The bottom line here is: Be cautious in mixing "church and state."

Following the Student's Schedule

When a student dies, the specific plan might be to have two adults follow the deceased student's schedule. This means at the beginning of each class period, two adults (these could be crisis team members, school counselors, school administrators, or combinations of these groups) would attend the class of the dead student.

The plan would be one of the adults would address the students from the front of the classroom and the other adult would sit in the deceased student's empty desk. The purpose of this would be to give students in the classroom the opportunity to share concerns, feelings, thoughts, and emotions with the people following the schedule, the classroom teacher, and their fellow classmates. Depending on the age of the students and the circumstances surrounding the crisis event, this can be an effective way to help students process various issues.

The rationale for sending two adults to the classroom is: To facilitate conversation (sometimes students are reluctant to talk and the two adults may have to dialogue between themselves until the students are ready to participate); to temporarily occupy the empty desk (this is an opportunity to directly observe who has been sitting next to the deceased student and gauge the impact the crisis may be having on those students); to provide assistance for each adult who is following the schedule (sometimes one of the people following the schedule may be overcome with emotion and will have to rely on the other adult to carry on the conversation with the class until he or she regains composure); and to be able to escort some students who need to go to the crisis center (the teacher or one of the adults following the schedule can do this without disrupting the classroom process).

Sometimes the adults following the student's schedule are in the classroom for only a few minutes and sometimes they remain throughout the class period. The length of time spent in the classroom is dependent on how the crisis is affecting the students and also on the particular classroom environment or climate. Students may feel more free to express themselves in certain classroom settings compared to those classrooms that have in the past been more restrictive to open discussion and dialogue.

Follow the classroom schedule throughout the day. In small school districts, the adults following the schedule may come into contact with all or most of the high school students by the end of the forth or fifth period. Experience has shown that if they stop following the schedule at that point, they miss opportunities to assist students even though they may have seen the same students earlier in the school day.

Telephones

Telephones, in the early stages of the response to a crisis, can be a problem. The problem can range from the disruptions they create when other issues need to be handled to the telephone being a source for inaccurate information leaking out to the media or the community.

Attention to detail is imperative throughout the crisis response and telephones and their appropriate use is crucial. Some control should be exercised in permitting access to telephones, especially early in the crisis response. Students should be discouraged from using telephones until after the school day has begun and the school/crisis team staff has had an opportunity to work with them.

The school secretary should be given a prepared statement to be used in response to incoming calls concerning the crisis. Some forms of the media will use the telephone to obtain the information for their news stories. Unless the school secretary has been trained as the school spokesperson for the media, he or she should not deviate from the prepared statement.

This conversation was overheard in a school office during a response to a crisis. The school secretary had just completed reading the prepared statement over the telephone when she realized she knew the caller, "Martha, is that you?" After receiving confirmation that Martha was indeed on the other end of the telephone, the conversation continued. "Martha, let me tell you what is going on around here!"

Parents who telephone the school concerning the crisis should have their concerns noted. Not all telephone calls need an immediate response, nor should the planned response be interrupted by telephone calls. A plan for prioritizing timely responses to telephone calls should be implemented and adhered to. Try to organize the telephone portion of the response so that the telephone becomes a helpful tool and not a dreaded problem.

More than one school district has felt the effect of a crisis that has occurred in another school district. The boy killed in the motorcycle/school bus accident or the critically injured girl may have relatives, friends, or other boyfriends/girlfriends in surrounding schools. There have even been instances where a student in a school across town or "down the road" has committed suicide after the death of a student in another school. Had the school staff been called and made aware of the situation, maybe an appropriate intervention could have been made and a confused and hurting young adult might still be alive.

Substitutes

A school district dealt with a crisis that resulted from a family feud over which television program the family would watch. One of the family members, a sixth grade boy, left the television room and went to his bedroom. Later when the family looked for him, they found him dead, hanging from a light fixture in his bedroom.

The school district's crisis team held a morning staff meeting the next day only to discover that after the meeting, eight staff members, acting separately, fled the school building and were not available to teach in their classrooms. Had the team planned, ahead and brought in two or three substitutes, another crisis would have been avoided. As it turned out, the crisis team had to abandon their specific crisis plan and cover the classrooms until substitutes could be called in to teach the classes.

It is not uncommon for staff and students to be affected by the "fight or flight" syndrome during times of crisis. Even if all staff remain on campus and cover their classes, substitutes can "float" throughout the school and provide teachers a few minutes relief from their classroom duties.

The Hospital

The specific plan should have a provision to deal with students or staff who may be critically injured (as was the case with the girl on the back of the motorcycle) or ill. Current, accurate, and up to date information is a major key to assisting students and staff when someone is in a hospital setting. The potential for rumors and incomplete information is considerable which often can lead to students and staff being on an emotional roller coaster.

Previous planning with hospital staff prior to a school tragedy is essential. Having a nurse on a crisis response team may be of some help. It is necessary that family, friends, and staff be focused on a "best case scenario" when it comes to critical injury or illness. However, it is also helpful if accurate and possibly "worse case scenario" information is obtained by the crisis response team so they can make appropriate contingency plans.

Student Initiated Responses

"What do you mean you aren't going to close school! We'll start a petition drive or better yet, we'll just walkout!!" (These words were uttered by a high school student council president after his good friend had killed himself with a shotgun in the school parking lot.)

Students, particularly at middle school and high school level, may decide they have a better plan for responding to the crisis than the specific plan being enacted. These reactions from students typically come in the early stages of the crisis response and need to be taken into account in your planning. Ignoring or not planning for student initiated responses can create another crisis. Sometimes this second crisis engulfs the original one.

What are student initiated responses? Examples include: Students wanting to close school in honor of a dead student; to have an assembly where they can eulogize the dead student; to dedicate the school yearbook in honor of the student; to retire the jersey of a dead student; to name a sports tournament after the dead student; to have a dead student's funeral at school; to hang a plaque/picture in the school in honor of the dead student; and others.

Student initiated responses are managed best by accurately anticipating students reactions to the crisis and responding with compassion, understanding, and careful listening. Avoid direct confrontation with students. If it is necessary to meet with some students who are challenging the way the crisis is being handled, meet with them individually or in small groups. The building administrator or a designate should conduct the meeting and, if possible, the crisis team leader should be present.

Be open to student questions, thoughts, and concerns. Students may be expressing ideas planted by parents and, in some cases, staff members. Students' reactions may be due to a lack of information or understanding of school policies or rules. Frequently, student reactions are based on emotions and the need to "just do something." Students usually respond favorably when they feel they are being heard and when they are presented with viable options. However, there are times when, in spite of everything, students are not accepting of anything except what they want. Although these situations can be unpleasant, these are times when schools need to follow their specific plan and not make adjustments they know are not in the best long term interest of the students, staff, and school district.

Student Possessions at School

The high school student who died in the motorcycle/school bus accident had, like most students, personal possessions in his locker(s). No matter the age of the students who have died, there should be a plan to deal with their possessions that are on school property.

High school and middle level students normally have a school locker assigned to them. This is their personal space, sometimes shared with an assigned locker mate or friend, to keep their "stuff," i.e., books, notebooks, coat or other clothing, and other personal items. Elementary students may have lockers, but they usually keep their possessions in desks in their classroom.

When a student dies, something needs to be done with the possessions at school. Although this can be handled in numerous ways, some methods seem to be more effective than others. (See Chapter 10.)

Sometimes school teachers and/or administrators remove all of the students possessions from lockers and/or desks. This is frequently done as an after thought and there may not be a specific plan in mind. This may be efficient and meet the needs of adults, but there are other options that meet the needs of everyone, including students.

The After School Meeting

Even though certified and classified staff met early in the morning after the motorcycle/school bus accident, and even though staff had an opportunity to informally communicate throughout the school day, it was important for staff to gather together after the school day. The after school meeting (see Chapter 6) is an opportunity to summarize the events of the day, respond to staff concerns, encourage support for each other, and review the plan for the next school day.

The building principal or a representative is in charge of the after school meeting. The day's events are briefly reviewed and, if necessary, deviations from the specific plan for the day shared at the early morning staff meeting are explained. Staff questions are answered and comments acknowledged, i.e., "It went better than I expected." "Did anyone talk to Travis Hill? He was really having difficulty in my third period class." "In thirteen years of teaching, I have never had a more exhausting day!" "I still think we should have called off school and just taken the day off."

If the motorcycle/school bus accident had happened during the noon hour instead of the evening before, the after school staff meeting may have been the first time the entire staff met. If this were the case, many of the items that would originally be covered in the early morning meeting must be a part of the after school meeting.

The meeting concludes with a review of the plans for the next day. If the crisis event has attracted media attention, the after school staff meeting can be used to caution staff about talking to the media. If the plan is to keep the building open in the evening, everyone is asked to encourage any students or parents who might contact them to make use of the services available to them at school that evening.

After a long day of responding to a crisis situation, it may be tempting to not have an after school meeting. Experience has shown these meetings, even though they do not last very long, are necessary to share information and "check on staff."

The Funeral

Many people go through life dreading one thing, their own funeral. Some may even discuss their "final plans" with family or friends. One thing is for certain, whether we plan for it or not, we will all have an opportunity to have a funeral.

The death of the high school student killed in the motorcycle/school bus accident was swift and sudden. As is usually the case with a young person who is killed in an accident, no prior plans had been made for the funeral.

The funeral (See Chapter 13) can be one of the most difficult aspects of crisis response. It is an event not under the school's control yet it affects many people. The time of day the funeral is held, the place where it is held, and the type of funeral may require changes in and create problems for the specific plan.

Well trained crisis response teams include funeral strategies in their specific plans. From trying to influence the time of the funeral (it is much better to have funerals after school hours); to trying to get parents to attend funerals with their students (in many instances the majority of adolescents attending funerals are not accompanied by an adult); to working with the person who may be preaching at the funeral (funerals that make dead students "larger than life" can create problems for the survivors); to many other issues, the school administration and the crisis response team can have a large role to play in helping plan for the funeral.

Memorials

"Let's dedicate the basketball season to the memory of Jason." "We need to put up a plaque in memory of Jeanette." "I hear that Jerry's parents have started a fund drive to purchase a trophy case and give it to the school if the school will retire his football number and put his picture in the center of the trophy case."

As implied in the section on student initiated responses, memorials can be a significant issue. School administrators and crisis response team members should anticipate this issue and, prior to the death of their next student or staff member, develop appropriate options for memorials.

A large percent of school buildings in this country have received memorials of some sort or other. Some of the memorials date back to World War II and maybe even before. America has a long history of remembering those who fought and died for their country as well as those who "just died."

Any type of memorial in a public setting, i.e., school buildings, makes a statement as to the values of the community. These value statements can and frequently do create problems for school crisis response teams.

Again, referring to the example of the motorcycle/school bus accident, suppose the boy who died was an excellent student academically, had superior athletic talent, was very popular with students, and came from a family of influence in the community. Imagine the ground swell of support that might occur after his death and the interest there would be in remembering him. One might assume, at the very least, somewhere in the school building would be some sort of tribute to the dead student, i.e., picture or plaque.

Suppose this same student, with all of his academic, athletic, and personal skills, was drunk when his motorcycle slammed into the school bus. What effect would this have on the community values and the decision to memorialize the student? What impact would a memorial have on other students and their values?

Suppose this talented high school student did not die as a result of an accident but, using a shotgun, killed himself. What concerns might that raise for remembering the student through some sort of memorial?

Suppose this student were not academically talented, but did poorly in school, was not held in high regard by many of his teachers, had very few friends, and had parents with no influence in the community. What are the chances this student would be remembered with plaques, pictures or the yearbook dedicated to him? Or, suppose the well liked/well positioned student dies in an accident and the school memorializes him and the not well liked/not well positioned student dies in an accident two years after the memorialized student and the school decides, for whatever the reasons, not to memorialize that student. Given these and many more possibilities, it does not take a fertile imagination to see the myriad of problems facing administrators and school crisis teams when it comes to memorials and their appropriateness.

This brief synopsis of the motorcycle/school bus accident and the design of a specific plan for the crisis has not addressed the issues resulting from: (a) the critically injured girl; (b) the comment made by the bus driver; (c) the fact the critically injured girl's sister was on the school bus; (d) the media's discovery the bus driver had previously received citations for speeding; (e) witnesses of the accident stating the motorcycle was traveling at a high rate of speed; (f) the father of the critically injured girl being on the school district's board of education; and (g) the superintendent and the high school principal being out of state attending a national conference. All of these circumstances, and possibly more, would need to be considered and included in the design of the specific plan.

After Thoughts

Even though there are some specific and basic constructs to school crisis response, let's explore why some of them don't always work the way they should.

Verify Information

Under the best of circumstances, it is sometimes difficult to obtain detailed and accurate information after a crisis event. Mistakes in this arena include:

- Failure of the school and/or the crisis team to establish a working relationship prior to a crisis with those who possess sensitive information during a crisis (law enforcement, fire and rescue personnel, and other legal entities).
- Ineffective measures of rumor control.
- Lack of someone on the crisis team who is proactive, tenacious, and conscientious in seeking verification information.
- Inappropriate timing between when the crisis event occurs and the activation or involvement of the school crisis team.
- Inordinate attempts by school officials to control the crisis response.

Calling Tree

With appropriate planning, one would think that a school's calling tree would be an effective way to notify staff of an emergency or crisis event. Mistakes in this arena include:

- Not all staff are on the school's calling tree list.
- Indecision concerning a consistent way to deal with personal answering machines.
- Inaccurate information finding its way into calling tree as the "tree grows."
- Restriction by school officials of important information in the calling tree message.
- Delay in activating the calling tree.
- Confusion in calling tree protocol due to lack of use.

Notifying the Crisis Response Team

The school's crisis team is well trained and eager to assist, but they are not called to respond. Mistakes in this arena include:

- Lack of a clear definition of what constitutes a school crisis.
- Inadequate planning for effectively contacting crisis team members 24/7.
- Improper chain of contact structure for the crisis response team.
- School officials do not activate the crisis response team.
- Less than effective crisis response team leadership.

Crisis Team Meeting

A well thought out specific crisis response plan requires concentrated thought, input from all team members, and a sufficient amount of time to formulate an effective response plan. School crisis teams will need to meet prior to their direct response to formulate the specific crisis plan. Mistakes in this arena include:

- Crisis team does not have adequate practice in putting a plan together quickly.
- Crisis team does not meet prior to responding to the school.
- School officials exercise control over the formulation of the crisis response plan.
- Delay in contacting the team and a hurried response required.

Meeting with Administrators

School administrators are just that, school administrators. They are responsible for administrating the day in and day out operations of a school where quality teaching and learning occur. During a school crisis, the quality of the teaching and learning can be impacted and, depending on the duration of the school crisis, may deteriorate.

As school leaders, and because of the nature of their leadership role, school administrators need to be closely involved with the crisis response. They also need to have reasonable control over the plan that is devised to assist them and their school in dealing with the crisis at hand. It can be a fine line to walk for administrators and crisis team members as they hammer out an appropriate plan to manage the school crisis. Mistakes in this arena include:

- Crisis team tries to take total control of the crisis response.
- School administrators are left out of the information loop and are not aware, or they are kept unaware, of the crisis plans as they evolve during the crisis response.
- School administrators try to control the crisis and the efforts of the response team.
- School administrators do not delegate authority to associates and others who may be helpful in organizing the crisis response.
- The principal of the building where the crisis has occurred is away from the community and there is little time or effort made to contact that person.

The Morning Staff Meeting

During a school crisis, having all school staff meet early in the morning, prior to the beginning of the school day, can be very helpful. It is an opportunity to share information, collect pertinent information from the staff, listen to concerns, and prepare people for the day ahead. Mistakes in this arena include:

- Staff meeting held too close to the beginning of the school day. During times of school crisis, schools should consider convening morning staff meetings at least one hour before school is scheduled to begin. Staff report the need to have some time to themselves or with fellow staff after such meetings, and before students enter the building, to begin their school day.
- School leadership is not present to lead the meeting.
- Confusion about the crisis event and exact details disturb or frighten staff.
- Not enough crisis team people are on hand to handle issues that come up.
- School staff is not familiar with the school district's crisis response plan and the overall concept for managing crisis events that impact the school.

The Announcement

During highly stressful times, people seek information. School crisis events can be very stress-filled. It stands to reason that relevant, accurate, and timely information is crucial if the students and staff are to successfully negotiate the crisis. Timely and informative announcements to students and staff are one of the bedrocks of school crisis response. Mistakes in this arena include:

- Announcements raise more questions than answers.
- Announcements are not heard by all students and staff.
- The main announcement is preempted by other announcements.
- Announcements contain inaccurate information and create rumors.
- Announcements are not made in a timely fashion.
- Announcements sound "canned."

The Letter

Communication! Communication! Communication! If the hallmark of a successful real estate transaction is location, location, location (and it is), communication is the hallmark of successful school crisis management. A major part of that communication effort should be directed to the parents and members of the community.

The drafting and distribution of a letter to the parents of students in schools impacted by tragedies has been, and will continue to be, a basic ingredient of school crisis response. Mistakes made in this arena include:

- Decision is made not to write a letter.
- Letter is given to students to take home and most letters don't arrive.
- School district does not want to spend the money to mail the letter.
- Letter contains inaccurate information.
- Letter does not allay fears.
- Letter does not contain information to aid parents in helping their children.

Crisis Rooms

Students and staff who choose to should have a designated place in the school building to visit with crisis team members. This "place" is often a crisis room or grieving room. Mistakes made in this arena include:

- The crisis room is not a comfortable environment in which people can talk and share.
- The crisis room is too far removed from main traffic areas of the school.
- A crisis room is not set up for school staff.
- Food and pop are served to the students in the crisis room and there is a party atmosphere.
- The crisis team does not have a predetermined plan or model for talking to people in the crisis room.
- The crisis room is open for several days, and students begin to take advantage of the situation.
- Staff has a lack of understanding regarding the purpose of the crisis room and make inappropriate remarks.
- The crisis room has to "change places" throughout the school day, causing grieving students to move through the halls several times.
- The crisis room is set up in a place where students need to go for instructional information, e.g., a media center.
- Students choose to create their own crisis room (in hallways, in front of a deceased students locker, outside) and crisis team staff have difficulty adjusting to the situation.

Using Mental Health Staff/Clergy for Crisis Response

There are a lot of helping resources available in many communities across our nation. During times of local or national tragedies, some of these resources may be brought to bear in helping schools better manage the tragic event. When I responded to the bombing of the federal building in Oklahoma City, many of that community's helping resources were harnessed and focused on people, young and old, needing help. High profile events can bring out the best, and occasionally the worst, in a community, state, or nation. School districts may call on helping resources in the community during times of crisis. Mistakes made in this arena can include:

- Some members of the helping community may not understand their role in a school during the response to a crisis event.

- Some community resources may not see themselves as a part of the school's crisis response team and "do their own thing."

- The helping resources may not see themselves as being able to assist the school for an extended period of time.

- Members of the helping community may need to continue offering their usual resources, thus causing their constituents to come to the school for assistance.

Following the Student's Schedule

Mainly in secondary schools, a successful strategy in school crisis response has been to have some of the crisis team members or other school staff follow the class schedule of students who have died or been injured in order to answer questions and/or facilitate discussion. In some instances, this procedure has been used when students are missing and their whereabouts or physical well being is unknown. Mistakes in this arena can include:

- Team members elect not to use the strategy.

- Teachers and administrators see it as an unnecessary disruption of class time.

- Crisis team members have not practiced proven discussion and interventions strategies in settings with large numbers of students, e.g., a classroom.

- There is a delay of a day or two before the procedure is attempted.

Telephones

Believe it or not, there was a time when cell phones did not exist. Those days are most certainly over. Not only are people able to communicate more easily, but they are able to share information almost instantly. Yes, the *wonders* of technology. Yes, the *problems* of technology. Telephones, cell or the old fashion ones, useful as they may be, may create problems for school officials and school crisis teams during times of tragedy or in the aftermath of tragic events. Mistakes in this arena can include:

- Allowing students to possess or use cell phones at school.

- Not having an up-to-date "map" of all phones in the school and monitoring their use at all times, especially during a crisis event.

- Relying on phones installed in classrooms to communicate information or to be effective/available during a school crisis.
- Through the use of cell phones, inaccurate and inappropriate information being leaked to the community.

Substitutes

Substitute teachers can provide needed additional resources during a crisis. It does make a difference *when* you call a substitute teacher during a time of crisis. Don't do it too late. Mistakes in this arena can include:

- Not having enough substitutes to cover classes.
- Not training substitutes in the basics of crisis response *before* the crisis event.
- Using substitutes to talk to students in the crisis room when the number of students overwhelms crisis team members.
- In the event of the death of a teacher, putting a substitute teacher in the deceased's classroom. Instead, put a teacher in the classroom that the students know and use the substitute to cover the other teacher's classes.

Chapter 5

The Announcement

No matter what the crisis event, it is often difficult to find an acceptable way to tell students/staff something bad has happened. The content of the announcement and the way it is "delivered" can have a major impact on the emotional reactions of the school community and even on the success of the school's entire response to the crisis event.

Tailoring the Announcement to Fit the Tragedy

At approximately 11:55 last night Bill Jensen's Bronco rolled at the intersection of 122nd and Fillmore County Line Road. Bill was able to struggle across a field for one-half mile until he came to a barbed wire fence. After resting for sometime, he managed to crawl through the fence and proceed another one-fourth mile to his home. He crawled into the detached garage and lay there until early morning when he was able to gather enough strength to make his way to the back door of his home. He kicked on the back door for about an hour until his mother heard a strange noise and called the police. The police found Bill Jensen at 4:35 a.m. and transported Bill to the hospital. Bill Jensen expired at 6:17 a.m.

This announcement was read over the intercom to high school students. Although the announcement gave specific details in regard to the death of Bill Jensen, it provided more information than students or staff needed, especially when an announcement was delivered over an intercom. Far too many details were provided and many of the details included may have been speculation rather than fact.

Each crisis event is unique and its impact on students and staff will differ. Tailoring the announcement to fit each tragedy is important. Designing an announcement prior to the crisis event or using a previous announcement and simply changing the details is not appropriate. Each tragedy deserves and requires an announcement designed to fit all of the circumstances that may arise and should be written to take into account the way it will affect all of the people associated with the school.

Helpful Hints on Making the Announcement

Contrary to the lengthy announcement about Bill Jensen's car accident and his death, the announcement should be kept short and to the point. Although students may want, and some may need, more information about the details of the accident, the complete details regarding the tragedy should not be included in the general announcement. A rule of thumb on content: Be honest, but don't be brutally honest.

If possible, try to add something to the announcement that will personalize it for the students. An example would be:

"We have something very sad to tell you. Mary Smith was driving to work last night and her car went off the road and hit a tree. Mary died in the accident. Her death was sudden, and she did not suffer." Pointing out that Mary did not suffer is a way of personalizing the announcement and should answer many student concerns about her death.

If at all possible, never tell staff and students at the same time about a crisis situation. If the event happens at night or on a weekend, a calling tree or early morning staff meeting will give you an opportunity to tell the staff. However, if an event occurs during the school day, it is important to let the staff know *before* the students are told.

Every means of communication has its unique problems. For instance, public address systems will let you inform all students at the same time and in the same way, i.e., they will all hear the same information in the same tone of voice. However, some school districts may think the public address system is too impersonal for announcements of this nature. In schools that do no have PA systems, this is not even an option.

If teachers make the announcement to the students, it can be more personal. It is possible students may hear the information in a variety of ways, even though the teachers are supposed to read from a preprinted statement. Students may also hear the announcement delivered with varying degrees of emotion or, lack of it.

If the principal or members of the crisis team choose to "make the rounds" and tell the students, frequently students in one classroom or section of the school building begin reacting to the information before other students have been told. In other words, no matter what method of announcing the crisis event to the students is used, any can create problems.

Regardless of the method used, crisis response team members should select certain classrooms to be in when the announcement is made. Rooms that may need crisis team members might include the dead student's classroom, classrooms where several of the dead student's friends might be, and classrooms where teachers have requested assistance in making the announcement to their students. If at all possible, close friends of the student should be contacted and brought together in a secluded location in the school and be told what has happened. Although you may not be able to contact all of the close friends, meeting with as many as possible should be helpful. This is also an opportunity to assist students who may be the most upset by the news.

Crisis team members should put on their "walking shoes" after the announcement has been made. That is the time to circulate throughout the building looking for trouble spots and offering assistance to students and staff. The crisis center (Chapter 9) should already be set up and staffed in anticipation of problems that may develop after the announcement is made.

If the announcement is made by the classroom teacher, facilitation questions should be included to assist teachers in processing the crisis event with the students. Examples include:

1. I'm having lots of mixed thoughts about this. What were your thoughts when you heard the announcement?

2. Do you plan to talk to adults at home about this? Who are the adults outside of school you can discuss this with?

3. If you have experienced losses in your own lives, how are you feeling now? Where are places you can go to discuss these feelings?

4. What can you do to help your classmates at times like this?

5. How did you first hear about what happened?

6. Where were you when you first heard about it?

7. When did you find out? What did you hear?

8. What did you first think when you heard about this?

9. What is the worst thing about this for you?

10. What is your greatest concern right now?

11. How did you feel when you heard about it?

12. What are you feeling now?

13. What gives you the strength to keep going?

14. What have you noticed that tells you things are getting better?

15. Who could you talk to about this when you go home tonight?

16. What are some things you can do for yourself to help you get through this?

17. Are there times when things aren't quite so bad? Describe that to me.

18. How can we help each other at a time like this?

Student/Staff Reactions

A crisis team leader once commented, "After the announcement is made, expect the expected and expect the unexpected, not only from the students but also from the staff."

A principal recalled, "After the announcement was made to the staff that one of our sixth graders had taken a rope and hanged himself, eight staff members fled the school building. They didn't get up and leave the staff meeting; but, between the time the staff meeting ended and the time school started, they left one at a time without the knowledge any of their colleagues were doing the same thing. Our second crisis of the day was trying to start school with eight teachers missing!"

A classroom teacher experienced this, "The students began to scream and cry. Some of the boys got angry and were hitting their fists against the wall. Although I asked they not leave, several students ran out of the room. Some even ran out the front door of the school building. In my years of teaching, I have never seen anything like it."

One of the most difficult times in the management of a school crisis is a period of time after the announcement has been made. This period of time will vary depending on the ages of students and staff, their previous experiences with losses in their personal lives, their various religious beliefs, and the popularity of the individual who has died.

Suggestions on having as much control of the situation as possible include:

1. Prior to making the announcement, get as much information as possible about students or staff who have experienced recent (within the past year or two) losses in their own lives. Be certain to follow up with these people as quickly as possible. If necessary, take them to a private supervised area of the school to hear the announcement.

2. Give staff the opportunity to obtain assistance in helping them make the announcement to students.

3. Remind the staff religious issues, especially in public schools, can be difficult to address and religion should not be discussed unless a student brings it up. Also, remind them to be accepting of all beliefs.

4. Remember individuals from various cultures may react differently and staff need to be accepting of all of these responses.

Some Things to Remember
About Making the Announcement

- Crisis teams should practice writing announcements for different crisis situations. If possible, one or two people from the crisis team who have expertise in this area should be appointed as the person(s) responsible to draft the announcement. Other team members should critique the announcement before the final draft.

- Preparations need to be made to accommodate those students who have already heard of the tragedy. These students may need additional assistance prior to the time the announcement is made to the entire student body.

- No matter how many students may have heard about the crisis situation, *always make the announcement.* It is important that each student/staff member hear the same thing. In most crisis situations, there are many people who have differing bits of information and there will always be rumors.

- You may need to write more than one announcement. For example, an announcement that a person is in critical condition may need to be updated if the individual's condition improves. Conversely, another announcement would need to be made if the individual dies.

- Keep the number of announcements to a minimum. Frequent announcements through the school day create an emotional roller coaster for students and staff and more problems for crisis team members.

- Remember, a large part of the success of the response to the crisis is dependent on how staff and students are informed about the crisis.

After Thoughts

All too often announcements are pre-canned. Crisis teams get out their manuals and turn to the page having one or more pre-written announcements. Then the job of changing portions of the announcement to fit the tragedy begins. Occasionally a name is filled into a blank and the task of "writing the announcement" is complete.

One might hope that after someone's death, others would begin with a blank sheet of paper and craft together words that might appropriately reflect that person's time on earth. Surely most of us hope, at least I do, that some person won't turn to a pre-written page, fill our name in a blank and then proceed to "announce" our demise. We all deserve better, and so do any students or staff members in your school district.

Always anticipate some students or even staff may not hear the announcement. Several months after doing a workshop, a school superintendent called to share regarding my comment, "While teachers may not read the announcement to students, this may occur in a large school district but not in a smaller one." He indicated he had only 23 certified staff members and knew all of them would share an announcement about a tragedy with their students. He went on to comment that a student from his school district had been killed in a car accident a couple of days prior to his call, and four of his staff did not read the announcement to their students. He said, "I just want to call and let you know it can happen, no matter what size school." He's correct.

If possible, strongly encourage teachers to dialogue with their students after they have heard the announcements. (Refer to the list of facilitative questions in this chapter on page 106.) Always remember staff is the front line of defense during a school crisis and often they are the best people to dialogue with students. Additionally, school crisis teams should consider writing facilitative questions for the staff *prior* to a tragic event. Have those questions available for immediate distribution to the staff. Tragic events on a local or national basis can occur during school hours, and school crisis teams may not be immediately available to assist students or staff. The tragic events in our nation of September 11, 2001 are an all too vivid example of teachers having to be on the front line with students as those harrowing events unfolded.

Chapter 6

The Before School/After School Staff Meeting

The meeting began at 6:30 a.m. All staff, certified and classified were in attendance. The silence was deafening. The principal thanked everyone for being there and began sharing the details of the car accident that killed the school's physical education teacher. "Last night around 9:15...."

Tragedies are seldom predictable in time, place, and victims. When they do strike schools it is important to inform the staff quickly and gather them together as soon as possible. For school district students and staff, it does seem that nights and weekends are the most vulnerable for tragic events. Therefore, it frequently is possible to have a before school staff meeting.

Notifying Staff

The importance of informing staff about a tragedy that impacts them and the school can not be overstated. It is crucial that schools have a plan in place to effectively contact all building personnel, i.e., certified staff, office staff, custodians, bus drivers, para-educators, and other classified staff.

The ease with which staff is contacted is dependent on the size of the school and the effectiveness of the contact plan. A commonly used procedure is a calling tree. A calling tree can be effective in getting basic information to staff in a short period of time, but is not very effective in accurately distributing detailed information. This is best managed at a staff meeting.

The calling tree (see Chapter 4), should include all staff. The list for the calling tree needs to be updated frequently and the "tree" should be activated at least once a semester to insure its efficiency.

Setting the Meeting Agenda

There should be a well thought out and organized agenda for the before school staff meeting. Frequently, this agenda is determined early in the morning at a meeting of the school's administrative team and members of the crisis response team. Some key agenda items include:

1. Current facts and details about the crisis event and dispelling rumors.
2. Introduction of the crisis response team and discussion of the team's role.
3. Outlining the plan for the school day and overview of the plan.
   a. How the crisis is to be announced to the students.
   b. Letter to parents.
   c. Availability of substitute teachers.
   d. Where/how crisis team members will be available.
   e. Location of crisis centers for students and staff.
   f. Guidelines for sending students to crisis centers.
4. Ideas for staff in dealing with students.
   a. Processing with students after the announcement.
   b. Using direct language, i.e., dead, died, killed.
   c. Being honest but not brutally honest.
   d. Moving into scheduled classroom activities.
   e. Dealing with a wide range of emotions.
   f. Working with students who feel guilty.
   g. Surfacing of feelings around unresolved losses.
   h. Handling inappropriate student remarks.
   i. Providing ways for students to express their feelings, i.e., artwork, cards, letter to the family.

5. Support for staff.

   a. Triggering of their emotions about their own previous losses.

   b. Dealing with their guilt, i.e., gave student a failing grade, didn't like the student.

   c. Let crisis team know if they need extra support in the classroom or personally.

   d. Substitutes available if needed.

6. Maintain normal routine as closely as possible.

7. Media

   a. Refer media to designated contact person (Announce the designated contact person).

   b. Discourage staff from talking to the media.

   c. Media personnel are not allowed inside the building.

   d. Discourage students from talking to the media.

8. Memorials—Review school policy if there is one.

9. Arrange to meet with teachers and other staff who work directly with the student(s) involved in the tragedy.

10. Announce plans for after school meeting if necessary.

Determining Who is in Charge

As simple as it may sound, determining who is in charge of the before school meeting might be an issue that can create a mini-crisis. The building principal is ultimately responsible for what occurs in the school. It would seem logical the principal should conduct the morning staff meeting. However, there can be extenuating circumstances which may require other people to assume responsibility for conducting the meeting such as: the principal is absent, the principal does not want to conduct meeting, or the principal is too emotional to conduct meeting.

Prior to the morning staff meeting, the crisis response team should have a meeting with the building administrator(s). It is at this meeting the general details and plans for the crisis response are decided. Topics and items that need to be covered at this meeting include:

1. Sharing the facts of the crisis event so administrators and teams members have the same information.

2. Planning the announcement to the student body.

   a. How will the announcement be made, i.e., intercom, written for teachers to read.

   b. When will the announcement be made.

   c. Drafting the announcement. (Written by crisis team member(s) and submitted to administrator for editing/approval).

3. Reviewing the letter that is to go home to parents.

4. Briefing office staff.

   a. Insuring no phone calls are made to the family regarding the student(s) not being in school.

   b. Procedures for reviewing the absence list for at risk students.

5. Identify and discuss:

   a. High risk groups, staff and students.

   b. Person who will be in contact with the authorities, i.e., police, hospital.

   c. Person(s) to be liaison with the family.

   d. Person to handle the student's belongings, i.e., locker, classroom desk(s), gym locker.

   e. Location for crisis center(s).

   f. Media contact person.

6. Delegate responsibilities.

   a. Person(s) in charge of staff meeting.

   b. Coverage of phones.

   c. Crisis center coverage.

   d. Covering special times and areas, i.e., playground, cafeteria, gym.

7. Review the outline for the staff meeting.

8. Substitutes.

   a. Obtain as necessary.

   b. Meeting with subs to brief them.

9. Identify any itinerant staff who need to be informed.

10. Plan for a meeting at the end of the school day.

11. Discuss memorials.

    a. Student initiated efforts.

    b. Parent efforts.

12. Notify surrounding schools.

13. Obtain staff/room list and/or building map for crisis team members.

When discussing item 6a (person in charge of staff meeting), it is vital the administrative team and the crisis team have a clear understanding as to their responsibilities in conducting the staff meeting and in working through the entire crisis event.

Some issues that need to be taken into consideration are:

1. Who is going to begin the before school staff meeting? If it is the principal, what is the plan if he or she breaks down or decides at the last minute not to conduct the meeting? This meeting sets the tone with the staff for the crisis response and needs, if at all possible, to "come off without a hitch."

2. Are their going to be shared responsibilities for conducting the staff meeting? If the principal and a person from the crisis team are going to co-lead the meeting, proper planning is necessary to insure the staff sees a smooth flow of leadership responsibilities. This is important because it reassures the staff the situation is under control.

3. What if the principal is unavailable to conduct the before school staff meeting? If at all possible, someone from the administrative team should be in charge of the before school staff meeting. Under most circumstances this should be the principal or a member of the school's administrative team. If a "stranger" to the staff conducts the meeting, it will make some of the staff uncomfortable and may create problems.

4. Who will handle the media? All crisis team members should have training in working with the media. Some school administrators may have training in working with the media. Although the decision as to the person(s) who will be working with the media during the crisis event might not be based entirely on training and expertise, consideration should be given to those who have had training and have demonstrated competence in this area.

5. Who should write the letter to be sent home to parents? The parent letter should be written by a member(s) of the crisis response team and submitted to the principal for approval/editing. (For information on the letter, see Chapter 12.)

Maintaining the Normal Routine

A question frequently asked by teachers is about the daily routine of school and the effect of the crisis event on that routine. Teachers may be unsure as to whether to proceed with their teaching plans for the day, whether to administer tests, and whether to continue with scheduled school and extracurricular activities. Guidelines and rationale regarding the maintenance of the normal school routine should be given to staff as opposed to permitting staff to determine their own guidelines.

Although the decision as to the maintenance of the normal routine of the school may vary in each crisis situation, some general guidelines may be applicable to any crisis event. These include:

1. School will be open for all students and will not be dismissed.
2. The schedule of extracurricular activities will be maintained.
3. Schools using bell schedules should maintain them. There may be some deviation in the bell schedule, i.e., need to extend class time to process information with students.
4. Attendance procedures should be maintained. In some instances it may be necessary to take attendance earlier than is normally done to determine whether "at risk students" are absent.
5. Teachers should, if at all possible, provide appropriate academic instruction for their students.
6. Guidelines regarding staff supervision of students, i.e., monitoring hallways, playgrounds, and parking lots should be maintained and, if appropriate, increased.

Many people, including students, thrive on routine to provide security and stability in their lives. When their routine is disrupted, their susceptibility to heightened emotion and concern may be increased. Maintaining as much routine as possible during a crisis event will benefit many students and staff.

At-Risk Staff Members

During some crisis response events, not enough attention is given to determining which staff members may be at risk and to providing an appropriate response to them. Being "at risk" does not focus on just some people; it can be a factor with anyone during times of crisis and stress. Care should be given to identify not only at risk students but staff as well.

Characteristics of staff who may be at-risk include:

1. Staff who have experienced recent losses in their personal lives. These may include losses due to death, divorce, moving, and missed career opportunities.

2. Staff who had the student(s) in their classroom. This may be particularity true if the teacher was: close to the student; feels the student missed opportunities because of the teacher; in the case of suicide knew that the student might attempt and did not disclose the information; or feels guilty about the way they treated the student.

3. Staff who have an undisclosed illness that may be terminal.

4. Staff who are in schools where several crisis events have occurred in a relatively short period of time.

5. Staff who are "loners" or not well accepted by other staff.

6. Staff who appear to have no support system in or out of the school setting.

7. Staff who have exhibited at risk behaviors previously, i.e., excessive use of alcohol or other drugs, suicide attempts or talk of killing themselves, or staff who have exhibited extreme behaviors.

8. Staff who have fled the school building and their whereabouts is unknown.

Crisis team members should have established procedures for identifying at risk staff and monitoring and working with them both during and immediately following the crisis event.

Working with Staff Directly Involved

Prior to the close of the before school staff meeting, crisis team members should plan to communicate with those teachers whose classrooms may be most directly affected by the crisis event. These teachers should have the opportunity to discuss their concerns and receive the assistance necessary to help them help their students.

Concerns teachers may need help with include:

1. Making the announcement to the students in their classrooms.

2. Processing the crisis event with their students after the announcement.

3. Helping students who were close friends of the dead student.

4. Helping students who have experienced recent losses.

5. Dealing with the possessions of the dead student.

6. Dealing with their own emotions while they are working in the classroom.

7. Talking with the parents of the dead student.

8. Attending the funeral.

9. Dealing with the student's empty desk.

10. Dealing with student comments, inappropriate remarks, delayed reactions, and no reactions.

11. Dealing with the students' fears of losing a parent, relative, or dying themselves.

Not only do crisis team members need to provide support in the classroom for teachers, they need to set up a "crisis room" for teachers who wish to come and talk to another adult about their feelings and concerns. This area should be away from the teacher work area/lounge. (See Chapter 9.)

The After School Meeting

Unlike the purpose of the before staff school meeting which is to set the "tone" for the day, the goal of the after school staff meeting is to bring some closure to the school day. It is an opportunity to review the day's events with the staff and receive or give new information. All of this is based on the premise the crisis event occurred before school started and there was an opportunity to have a meeting before school. There may be occasions, particularly if the crisis event occurs during the school day, when after school is the first opportunity to have a meeting with the entire staff. If that is the case, then many of the procedures described in the section on the before school meeting would apply to the after school meeting.

The after school staff meeting usually does not have a long agenda. Therefore, may be thoughts, particularly if the day has gone well, to not hold this additional staff meeting. This meeting will help staff. *Don't cancel it!*

Important agenda items for the after school staff meeting are:

1. Briefly reviewing the day's events.

2. Processing and validating the staff's feelings about the crisis.

3. Providing characteristics of high risk students.

4. Discussing students' reactions and identifying students the staff may have concerns about.

5. Discussing funeral arrangements.

   a. When and where.

   b. Procedures for staff who wish to attend.

   c. Procedures for students, i.e., students will need an excuse, students should be accompanied by an adult, and tests and other assignment make up issues.

6. Discussing staff concerns regarding support for the family.

7. Informing staff of the continued availability of the crisis response team and the crisis response plan for the next day(s).

8. Encouraging the staff to acknowledge and address their own emotional needs during the evening and in the days ahead.

9. Acknowledging the staff's efforts and thanking them.

It is important that crisis response team members strategically place themselves in the meeting room to assist staff if personal issues arise. Team members should do this at all staff meetings held during the time of the school crisis.

After Thoughts

Staff meetings may not be the greatest events, even during normal times. During highly stressful times, they may be difficult, at best. School crisis teams sometimes seem confused as to their role in planning, assisting, and conducting the staff meeting. Depending on the size of your school district and the number of crisis response experiences your district's team(s) have had, it is conceivable that response team members, particularly response team leaders, probably have more experience in designing and conducting a staff meeting during a school tragedy than many building administrators.

Crisis team members should be cautious about a preconceived paradigm for staff meetings during school crisis events. For example, a common concept is that the building principal would conduct the staff meeting. I can recall a response to a school crisis when I was looking for the principal just prior to the scheduled after-school-staff meeting. I inquired of office staff where the principal might be and was informed he was outside helping students board their school busses. Going outside, I approached the principal with the reminder the meeting was about to begin and that he had indicated in the after school meeting planning session that he had some items he wanted to share with the staff. The principal commented, "Can't you see I am busy putting children on their buses." Since all of the busses had departed the school about 30 minutes before, I indicated to the principal that it was my understanding all of the busses had left for the day. Upon hearing my comment, the principal replied, "Then I'll stay out here all night and wait for the first bus to return tomorrow, but I am not going to the staff meeting." Then the principal broke down and shared he had conducted too many of those types of difficult meetings and he could not do it again. Although most school crisis plans indicate an administrator should conduct and be a major participant in a school staff meeting, particularly during a crisis event, it may not be possible.

Talking to teachers over the years, it has become evident school administrators and crisis team members should consider the timing of school staff meetings during a school crisis event. If at all possible, a morning staff meeting convened because of a tragedy impacting the school, should be held at least one hour before classes are scheduled to begin. School staff consistently report they do not like being dismissed from the meeting, only to walk into the halls or their classrooms and have students in the building. Staff members would like to have some time and space to reflect on their emotions and prepare themselves to have the best interactions possible with their students.

One staff meeting agenda item commonly neglected by crisis teams is direction to staff on various classroom instructional protocols during a crisis event. Staff should receive specific suggestions on how they might best blend assisting their students in dealing with the tragedy and providing appropriate instructional experiences. In this technological age, crisis teams should assist administrators in formulating appropriate suggestions for staff. Particular attention should be paid to the use of live television broadcasts, if the crisis impacting the school is being covered by the television media. It is appropriate to caution staff about exposing their students to live media events. All of us can remember space shuttle tragedies, terrorist attacks, and media coverage of wars when we experienced unexpected images of destruction and death. A conscious decision needs to be made as to whether school staff will be allowed to permit their students to watch live media coverage of breaking news tragedies.

Chapter 7

The Reaction
of Staff/Students

Six-year-old Jennifer, "My Mom said that my grandpa got sick, went to the hospital and died. So, I'm never going to get sick and then I won't have to go to the hospital and die."

Eleven-year-old Donald, "Jeremy was my best friend before he died of cancer. We used to be together all the time, and every once in a while we drank out of the same glass. I'm afraid I'm going to get cancer from Jeremy."

Sixteen-year-old Harold, after his brother died in a car accident, "Only the good die young. I'm going to be one mean SOB."

Forty three-year-old Diane, "Every once in awhile God needs a good little boy or girl in heaven and that is why He came and took Susan."

The reactions of students and staff, when grief visits school, may be as varied as the total number of students and staff in the school. This reaction may then be multiplied and influenced by the number of people outside the school setting who come into contact with students and staff. Additionally, the reactions may vary, based on previous grief experiences in the lives of students, staff, and those with whom they have contact. It is little wonder crisis response teams can have a variety of problems dealing with the reactions of students and staff during times of tragedies.

The Staff

When crisis response teams are called into a school, information they need from administrators include the names of staff, certified and classified, who have had recent losses in their lives. These could either be losses through death, divorce, or children who have recently left home. Information should also be gathered regarding serious illnesses in families or staff who are dealing with family or friends who are terminally ill.

Many people who have experienced loss in their lives, especially through death, indicate there is no such thing as grief recovery. They describe it in terms of reconciliation of the loss, but they never completely recover.

When tragedy strikes a school, some of the staff who have experienced previous losses may actually regrieve those losses. This re- grieving process may take many forms. The important thing for the crisis response team to consider is this regrieving process may limit the ability of some staff members to effectively help students and other staff members who are experiencing grief.

If crisis response teams have specific information about losses in the lives of some of the staff, they need to take that into consideration as they develop their specific response plan. Part of the plan may be to anticipate regrieving by certain staff members and prepare to respond to them if the opportunity presents itself.

Teams also need to be aware that some staff will experience difficulty during times of tragedy, even if they have had no significant losses in their lives. For example, a staff member may experience problems during the event simply because he or she has a child the same age or sex of the student who has been killed. As a caring parent who deeply loves one's own child, the staff member may experience difficulty in handling the crisis event.

Unfortunately, even though team members receive some information about staff, they generally do not have complete information on all staff members that may have "loss" issues. No one is at fault when this occurs. Some people choose not to share issues in their private lives, so no one in the school would be aware of problems that might occur with them. For example, in a school where a crisis response team was responding to the death of a teacher, an excellent specific response plan had been designed and implemented. However, shortly after school was in session, one of the crisis team members was walking down a hall when she noticed a room full of kindergarten students did not have a teacher present. She inquired among the students as to where their teacher was and several of the students pointed to the closet door in the classroom. When the crisis team member opened the door, she found the classroom teacher lying on the floor in a fetal position, sobbing. The crisis response team later learned the teacher who had died was the cooperating teacher for the kindergarten teacher when she was doing her student teaching. No one connected with the school recalled this relationship and the kindergarten teacher did not share with anyone she was having difficulty with the teacher's death.

Another example, alluded to earlier, was a group of eight teachers who "fled" from a school that was dealing with the death of a sixth grade student who hanged himself after a family argument over what television program the family was going to watch. These teachers left the school one at a time and without any awareness anyone else was leaving. All of them had experienced losses in their personal lives and the death of the sixth grade student triggered a regrieving of these losses.

These are two out of hundreds of examples of crisis response teams and school administrators having to make significant adjustments in their specific crisis response plans because of the reaction of staff during a school tragedy. Sometimes these situations can not be avoided, but they might have been less traumatic for everyone if team members had advance knowledge of previous grief experiences with staff. A positive side to this is the opportunity to assist staff if these previous experiences come to the forefront during the crisis response. These examples should also serve as a reminder to have a "crisis room" for staff other than the faculty study or teacher's lounge.

The Students

"When the going gets tough, the tough get going." Some segments of American society place a high value on being strong during difficult times. Even when someone close to us dies and our lives have been changed forever, we may be expected to not take very long in "getting on" with life. Many adults hold onto grief for sustained periods of time even though some may not find it acceptable or healthy. It is little wonder, then, that some adults have difficulty understanding the grieving process and grief patterns of children and adolescents.

When grief visits school, students may not grieve in predictable patterns and this may create issues that hinder managing the crisis. "Look kids, nobody ever said that life was easy and you would get by without a few lumps." "You guys are just a bunch of cry babies." "This is math class, not Dear Abby class!" "If I wanted to be a school counselor, I would have bought a box of tissues. This classroom is not a counseling office!" These types of comments from staff usually reflect frustration and a misunderstanding about young people and grief.

The early morning staff meeting, if it is possible to have one, is usually the first opportunity to visit with staff about the way the team expects the students to respond to the crisis situation. This is the time to acquaint staff with typical grieving behavior at various developmental stages.

Some behaviors staff might observe are:

Children (5 to 11 Years)
Shock/denial

Anger, aggressive behavior

Guilt

Idealization of the dead student/adult

Sleeping/eating problems

Headaches/stomach aches

Withdrawal

Sadness

Poor concentration

Unwarranted fears/worries

Acting younger than their age, i.e., whining, clinging

School phobia or avoidance

Adolescents (12 to 18 years)
Shock/denial

Anger/aggressive behavior

Rebellion at school/home

Feelings of guilt

Fighting, withdrawal, attention seeking

Poor concentration

Loss of interest in peer/social activities

Lack of feelings

Decline of interest in the opposite sex

Sadness

Idealization of the dead person

Restlessness

Completely consumed by the situation

Giddiness/laughing/joking

(Wolfelt, 1983.)

The mix of behaviors listed above give a hint as to some problems that may arise in helping young people with their grief. One student may exhibit several of these behaviors at the same time. Other students may be more consistent in their behavior patterns. And yet another student may not outwardly show any sign of grieving. "I cry all the way home from school and all the way to school, but I don't let anyone see me cry at home or at school," said a seventh grade boy. "I talk to Melissa every night when I go to bed and tell her how much I miss her, but I don't tell anyone about it," related a high school junior girl. "I really miss my dad. I sure wish I could talk to someone but if I do, they might tell my mom and that would make her cry again. I want to be strong for her so I don't talk about him and I never cry," shared a third grade boy.

Staff should be reminded students frequently act out their feelings instead of talking about them. Some students might be loud and argumentative while others might want to be left alone and not interact with anyone. Others may be so overwhelmed they revert to younger child like behaviors and won't "act their age."

Some students will have no reaction and may feel guilty their friends are grieving and they are not. Early adolescents may decide to grieve because their friends are grieving. Students from various backgrounds and cultures may express their grief in ways unfamiliar to staff and other students. (See References, pages 223-224, for contemporary articles/books on children/young people and grief.)

It is important to give students the opportunity to acknowledge and discuss their feelings. This can be best facilitated by adults in the school by acknowledging their own feelings. A comment like, "My feelings are all mixed up right now, and I think each of you is probably having all sorts of feelings. I want to hear what you're thinking. I'll try to answer any questions you have as best I can." When adults share their feelings, i.e., sadness, emptiness, confusion, fear, and anger, it helps students see grieving is a natural response to losses. Plus, it reminds students the staff in schools are real people.

When students do express their feelings, it is very important these feelings be acknowledged. Students need to feel their thoughts and concerns are important. Adults may try to cheer up students or bring up other issues to distract students from their feelings. Students need to be listened to and have their feelings acknowledged.

School is the Place to Be

Some school districts choose not to give students the opportunity to share their feelings with staff by electing to close school during all or a portion of the crisis event. The decision to close school or cancel school activities is frequently a misunderstanding by staff and/ or adults in the community that the way to show respect is to not maintain routine and to cancel events. Closing school, coupled with a lack of understanding of young people and how they grieve, can create additional crises for students.

During a crisis students need and rely on structure. They welcome, although they may act like they don't, the security of something familiar to them even if it is school bells ringing and classes in session. When this structure is taken away, they often feel their lives, coupled with the crisis situation, are out of their control. This may be especially true if, in the case of a student's death, the entire school is dismissed for the funeral of the student. Although mental health professionals generally agree going to a funeral can be a positive experience and a way for students to say good-bye, they should not feel pressure to attend the funeral. Dismissing school for the funeral may also be an indicator to students and parents the school is encouraging attendance at the funeral. (See Chapter 13 on funerals.)

If a crisis occurs when school is not in session, i.e., at night, on a weekend, over a short vacation period, or during the summer, it may be necessary to open the school for students, staff, and parents. Crisis response team members and/or other school staff members should be available at the school to assist young people and adults who seek help. Many school districts have reported positive results and have usually been surprised at the large numbers of students who take advantage of this opportunity to come to school for help.

It is not unusual for school officials to receive phone calls from parents during times of crisis informing the school students are "gathered together" at someone's home or local student hangout. In order to provide crisis team support for these students, parents should be encouraged to have their students come to the school. Sending school staff and crisis team members to various sites away from the school campus can dilute the effectiveness of the crisis response. Additionally, it may make communication between the crisis team and school staff difficult and sometimes impossible. "School is the place to be," a slogan from a Midwestern school district, may never be more true than during a school crisis.

After Thoughts

Teachers are very important to their students. From them, students learn, not only facts and figures, but behaviors and emotions. School is a home away from home, a place for students to share their lives with others. During a crisis impacting the school and when students are grieving, they need to share their feelings with someone they trust. Often times that "someone" is a teacher.

To help students cope with death and grief, we must continually enhance our own knowledge of childhood grief. While we never have all the answers, we can always strive to broaden our understanding and degree of helpfulness.

Another part of learning about grief involves exploring your assumptions about life and death. Think about your own personal losses. What person close to you have died? What did their deaths mean to you? Were you a child when someone you loved died? If so, how did you feel? How did the important adults in your life, including your teachers and other school staff, help you with your feelings of grief? Thinking about these experiences and issues will help you better help the students under your care.

Students frequently grieve in doses. They take in only what they can handle at the moment. Then they may take a break from their grief by playing or engaging in other daily activities. Later they may come back with more questions or expressions of emotions. This does not mean they don't care or are too young to understand. This is their way of processing a difficult situation. Your students may be less able than adults to put feelings into words, so their grief may be seen in their behaviors. Some students express the pain of grief by acting-out. This behavior usually varies, depending on the student's age and developmental level. Some students may temporarily display regressive behaviors, reverting back to a safer time in their lives. Young students may not even understand the permanence of death.

Older students often have a more adult understanding of death, but they may not fully accept that it will happen to them. A common characteristic of young students is the belief in their own immortality. During school tragedies, it is not uncommon for older students to seek out support from their friends and peers. This type of support is important, but these students also need caring support from the teachers and other school staff.

Although students and staff may have various reactions during school crisis events, some suggestions in helping young and old during tragic events include:

- Be honest—If you don't know information, say so. Even younger students are experts at sensing when adults are being truthful.

- Use clear language—Don't use euphemisms to explain death. Use words like dead, died, killed.

- Validate questions—Don't dismiss or gloss over student or adult concerns. Validate people's concerns. Using words like, "You will understand when you are older" or "You have to be strong" is not helpful.

- Be available—In your absence, the student will most likely supply his or her own interpretation and answers, which may not be realistic or healthy.

- Be reasonable—Take into account developmental differences in the students. Whether a student understands time or can think logically determines his or her ability to cope with the crisis event and the fact some students or adults have died.

- Do listen—Be a good listener. Listen to the concerns of students, letting them know no question is too silly or too terrible. Don't be judgmental.

- Be direct—Ask what truth the students are seeking. Don't assume they want a lot of information if a simple fact will do.

- Be there—Show your support by being there, even if you do nothing but sit with the students. Loneliness is one of the most difficult aspects of loss for young and older students and even adults.

- Be open to religious beliefs—Recognize that different people believe different things. Be respectful of those differences. Allow discussions on religion, but do not initiate them.

- Be resourceful—Allow students to express emotions in their own way including drawing, writing, music, and so forth.

Chapter 8

The Problems of Under/Over Responding

"Everything is OK here." "I don't think many of the students will have any problems." "We went through one of these six years ago and everything eventually worked out." "We can tough this out." "Today's Friday and the students won't be here 'til Monday. Maybe they'll forget it by then." "Oh, maybe we could use just a couple of extra people for a little while." "This happened when I was in a smaller school district and even though I have four times the number of students, what worked before should work again." "Let's try it on our own for the first few hours and if we get in a mess, we'll call the crisis response team."

Accurately Assessing the Crisis

If you are going on a long hike in the mountains on a day the weather forecaster predicts severe storms, remember to take plenty of clothes and dress in layers. If the weather is as predicted, you will be fine. If the weather is better than predicted, you can remove some of the layers of clothing. But if you are not prepared and the weather gets worse than you anticipated, at best you might get cold and wet. At the very worse you might get hypothermia and maybe die. More than one school district has become hypothermic and been near death during a crisis event. The "near death" has been witnessed by the media, the community, the parents, the staff, and even the students. The result is frequently a much larger problem with the crisis or a series of mini-crises.

A common problem in crisis response is accurately predicting how severe crisis situations really are. As a result, schools frequently either under or over respond to the crisis event. Experience has shown it is better to over respond than under respond.

Response Opportunities

One of the basic crisis mistakes schools make is not considering the possibility of a response at all. Crisis teams often confess they didn't even get together to discuss whether a response was appropriate or not. Sometimes they don't get together because no one calls them to let them know something has happened. The administration of the school may decide they don't think they need a response and so the team isn't called. At other times the crisis team leader makes an autonomous decision not to respond and doesn't call the team members together; or it is just to inconvenient to get the team together, i.e., weekends, holidays, and summer vacation.

Crisis response teams should always meet and discuss the options available to the school district in any crisis situation. They should remember the opportunity portion of the Chinese definition of crisis (dangerous opportunity) and look for opportunities that are inherent in almost every crisis event.

Let's look at some crisis situations that could happen in any school district no matter the size and consider some possible response opportunities.

Even though people do not die in order, it is not uncommon that a student's grandparent will be the first human death the student will experience. Opportunities at these times include: (a) informing the student's teacher(s) about the grandparent's death; (b) offering the teacher(s) information on how young people grieve; (c) offering to assist the teacher in a classroom discussion about the situation (frequently the death affects more students than just the one who is experiencing it); (d) offering the teacher(s) information about other students in the class who have had other loss experiences (schools, with the assistance of the crisis team, should keep up-to-date records of loss experiences students have had over the years); (e) encouraging the teacher to have students who wish to express their concerns for the student to do so through writing or art work; (f) encouraging the teacher(s) to dialogue with the class about appropriate comments to make to the student and encourage the class to share what they think the student might be feeling. All of this may help the student whose grandparent has died, it may also help other students in the class who have had a loss through death and perhaps better prepare some of them for a future loss.

Consider the situation of a student with only a few friends who is terminally ill and has been absent from school for several weeks or months before his death. The rationale for a limited response or for not responding at all usually is that the student was not well known or that he had not been in school recently. Missed opportunities in not responding include: (a) the possibility that some students in the class might fear, because of their contact with the student before his illness, that they will contract the disease, become ill, and die just like the student; (b) the guilt that some students may have that they did not try to get to know the student very well and may even have avoided him or made fun of him; (c) the concern of students who have parents or siblings who are ill and their fear about them dying; (d) the guilt that some students still carry because they had a friend or relative who died after a long illness and there were times they wished, for whatever reasons, that the friend or relative would die; (e) the fact this is another opportunity for some students to regrieve losses in their lives and they will do this whether someone is there to help or not.

Students Who are No Longer in School

Schools are sometimes unsure as to how to respond to the death of a student who is no longer attending the school, i.e., a graduate, a student who has moved to another school district, a student who has chosen to discontinue attending school or the school has excluded the student from attending. Responses to these circumstances may vary, but the crisis situation should not be ignored. Sometimes the death of a former student may cause a more significant reaction on the part of students and staff than the death of a student who is currently attending the school.

Student Popularity

Equity is important in every facet of a student's life. It is of equal importance in responding to a tragedy involving a student. When a student dies or is critically injured or ill, friends and family should receive the best crisis response the school has to offer. Schools will usually find, however, the more popular or highly visible the student, the greater the impact on the overall student population.

A mistake schools frequently make in their level of response during a crisis involving a student is misjudging the effect on the student population. It might be expected the death of a student who is not well known might not greatly influence the student body. Thus, a decision might be made to provide a scaled down crisis response. This decision might be correct. Keep in mind, however, the circumstances of the tragedy, the volatility of the student population, and even the time of year may have considerable bearing on the overall impact on the student population. Again, it may be more prudent to prepare for a major response effort and, if necessary, scale back the response as the situation unfolds.

Building Politics

Crisis response teams that have a high rate of success in effectively helping schools during a crisis have learned the fine art of working in every conceivable situation and circumstance. Translated, that means they have learned to be political, yet not compromise the effectiveness of the response.

Suggestions for successfully working through building politics include:

1. Be open and honest with the administrative team and the staff.
2. Keep the crisis team's focus on what is best for the students and staff.
3. Adhere to ground rules set by the principal. (If the team has done its "homework," there should be few if any areas of misunderstanding between the team and the principal about the design and implementation of the response to the crisis.)
4. Always negotiate for what will be in the best interest of the students.
5. If at all possible, attempt to work out win-win solutions.
6. Remember school tragedies are usually highly emotional and stressful times. Be as calm as possible and dust off your best listening skills.

Dr. John Dudley

School and building politics, or whatever term you would like to use, may and probably will be a key ingredient in determining the right degree of response. If necessary, always plan to over respond, i.e., a complete team and a complete response plan. The crisis team can always reduce the degree of the response once there has been a first hand opportunity to assess the situation.

Weekends, Holidays, and Vacations

Probably the biggest factor in under responding is the time the crisis occurs. Weekends, holidays, and vacations may affect the level of the response. No matter the day or time of year, it is important to respond as immediately as possible.

This means that response teams will need to have a system in place to contact its members during "non-school" times.

After Thoughts

The problems of *under* or *over* responding to a school crisis, important as they are, are not nearly as important as the problem of *not* responding. I am continually surprised at the number of school crisis team members I meet in my workshops who share instances when grief came to visit their school and their crisis team did not respond.

Excuses I frequently hear in an attempt to justify a schools lack of appropriate response to a tragedy impacting learning in the schools vary from, "We couldn't get our team together"; "It happened during the summer"; "We didn't think it would impact very many students"; "They were not very popular students"; to "I think we may have done something, but no one called me"; "Our new superintendent doesn't believe in school crisis response teams"; "He was a new student in our school district"; and "We didn't think a national tragedy would impact our students."

School crisis response teams should strive for equity in their response planning. If one student or staff person in your school district deserves a response, *all* students and staff deserve responses.

Contacting crisis teams, no matter the time of day, week, or year, should be made as practical and easy as possible. No matter the size of the school district, consideration should be given to using pagers to contact team members and to inform them of the need for their expertise. Costs for pagers have decreased dramatically over the past few years. School districts experiencing budget issues should give consideration to asking patrons and businesses in the community to assist in defraying pager costs. Most communities have access to an answering service, and often times these companies will dedicate a phone line to the school district's crisis response program. School administrators frequently share that the use of paging systems has made contacting their crisis response teams much easier, increasing the likelihood of teams being activated during tragic events that impact students, faculty, and other school staff members.

Chapter 9

The Crisis Center

"At one time during the day there were over a hundred students in the crisis room. Some cried; some laughed; some were silent; some were boisterous; some needed to be there; some needed to be in class. It was an experience!" (Comment after a crisis team member's first response.)

Location of the Crisis Center

The time to decide where to "house" grieving students during a crisis event is now, not when the crisis happens. Too often schools scramble to find places to send students who need help with grief issues. Or, schools question the need to have a student crisis room and, when something happens, they rush to find a place, any place, to work with students.

School administrators should plan where they would work with students who are significantly impacted by a crisis event. Commonly, these places are called crisis rooms and range all the way from classrooms to playgrounds and school yards. The crisis room is simply a place set aside for grieving students to gather.

Preferred places for crisis rooms are areas of the school not in the main student traffic pattern and which do not cause a disruption of the student schedule. For example, if the crisis room for students is in the media center, other students who want to use the school's media resources to complete an assignment will be unable to do so.

Some schools choose the counseling center as the designated crisis room. Again, students coming to the counseling center for assistance on issues other than the crisis situation, may not be able to get the information they need. Most counseling centers are also limited in size and will not accommodate large numbers of students.

When setting up a crisis room, try to set up an area of the school with sufficient space to take care of the number of students anticipated. Frequently, schools use classroom or auditorium space. A major consideration in the selection of a crisis room is an area that can be used throughout a school day or, if necessary, throughout the crisis situation which does not require the relocation of students.

Another consideration in the selection of a crisis room is an area of the school with some degree of privacy. Crisis rooms in open areas or in areas that have a lot of glass should be avoided if possible. Not only is the more private area helpful for students, it helps keep "on lookers" away.

As previously mentioned, teachers should also have an area in the building they can go to share and express their feelings. Experience has shown this should be a room other than the teachers' study or lounge.

The crisis room should have drinking water and several boxes of facial tissues available for students. If possible, the room should accommodate working with students in small groups. The down side of using a school auditorium, unless you use the stage, is the seating is usually stationary and it is difficult for students to cluster in groups.

Staffing the Crisis Center

Some members of the crisis team staff should be in the crisis room. The number of staff needed in the room is usually dependent on the number of students in the room. Sometimes the crisis team staff is augmented by building staff, i.e., counselors. The mix of staff and the numbers needed are usually determined by the magnitude of the crisis event. A rule of thumb is no more than three members of the crisis team in the crisis room at the same time.

Factors to Consider

Students need to be directed to the crisis room in a timely and orderly manner. Teachers should be asked to refrain from sending large numbers of students from their individual classrooms to the crisis center. If a large number of students in a particular classroom are having problems related to the event, crisis team members should be dispatched to the classroom to assist the teacher in working with the students.

A listing should be kept of all students who come to the crisis room. If necessary, an attendance record might be kept and that information shared with the administrative office. At all times, and especially during crisis situations, the school needs to know the whereabouts of all of the students enrolled in the school. Not knowing where students are may create problems. For example, a school district experienced a crisis when one of their high school students burned to death in a house fire. The response team organized and delivered an immediate response to the school. During the early stages of the response several students who were sent to the crisis room by teachers left the high school instead of going to the crisis room. Crisis team members called the parents of these students and, in many cases, talked directly with the students who had left school.

These efforts were successful and many students returned to the school. However, some of the students chose not to return or their parents decided to have them remain at home. Tragically, one of the students who did not return to school committed suicide that same day.

A frequent concern of staff about crisis rooms is when some of the students in the crisis room really do not need to be there and are taking advantage of the situation. That is probably a correct assessment. The difficulty comes in correctly identifying which students should be excluded from the crisis room.

Students come to the crisis room for a variety of reasons. Many are there because they are having difficulty dealing with the crisis situation. Some are there because their friends are having difficulty dealing with the situation and they want to provide support. A few are there because the crisis situation has triggered emotions and reactions to previous loss experiences. Others are there as onlookers and some are there because it is better, in their judgment, than being in their classrooms.

A natural sorting out process usually occurs in the crisis room and most students end up being "where they should be," i.e., in their classrooms, working with staff in small groups, or at home with an adult. Debating the appropriateness of some students being in the crisis room is usually not productive. Simply acknowledging the majority of the students in the crisis room are seeking assistance and a few are taking advantage of the opportunity should be sufficient in the defense of this important tool of crisis management.

Generally, a crisis room for students is only open during the first day of the crisis event. In some situations, it may be necessary to reopen the room if a second tragedy occurs during the response to the initial event. It may also be appropriate to open the crisis room after a student or staff funeral, particularly if a significant number of students attended the funeral. Crisis team members and school administrators should closely monitor the effectiveness of the crisis room in the overall response to the event and make a joint determination regarding the length of time it should be open to assist students.

After Thoughts

In Chapter 4, I discussed some common mistakes I see in the setting up and running of school crisis response rooms during a crisis. In my experience, one of the "things" school crisis teams do during their response to a school tragedy is to set up a place for students (don't forget staff) to go and talk about the issues they may be having as a result of the event.

School crisis response should be mindful of the fact crisis response rooms may not be a necessary part of the crisis response arsenal for certain school tragedies. Response teams might wish to decide, depending on the event and what they determine will be the impact on students and staff, to avoid setting up crisis response rooms. There may be some situations where students are better off remaining in their classrooms and have teachers and response team members work in that setting. Experienced teams should be able to determine when a change in the school's routine may have a negative impact on the students and decide not to set up crisis response rooms. In the event of the death of a high school student, teams may find it more valuable and effective to follow the student's class schedule, as opposed to setting up a crisis room.

Additionally, some school settings and environments preclude the ability to set up an effective place for students to come and talk. "Shoehorning" school crisis response rooms into that type of school setting may prove to be detrimental and not in the best interest of the students those rooms are designed to serve. In those situations, school crisis response teams may need to rely on the school's staff to provide not only frontline assistance for students, but most of the direct assistance for the students in the school. In such instances, the crisis team(s) may need to provide specific information for staff to assist students including such hints for teachers as:

- Take cues from your students about how much class time they need to talk.

- Often times there may be rumors or speculations when a student or staff death occurs. If you hear these rumors, discourage them. Remind students to stick to the facts and be respectful of the person who has died.

- While some students will be directly affected by the crisis event, others may not be. Some students may be indirectly affected, meaning this news may cause them to revisit deaths and other losses they have experienced.

- Everyone grieves differently. You may see a variety of responses in your students. Some may react by making comments or gestures that you may feel are inappropriate. These responses usually come from how uncomfortable they are with the situation. Help students be accepting of all grief responses.

- Please do not hesitate to let crisis team members know of any students who seem to be experiencing difficulty, especially if they have not sought help.

- Be aware of your own experiences with death and loss and how you may be affected by this situation. It is okay to share your feelings with your students and find healthy ways to take care of yourself.

Chapter 10

The Possessions
of the Students

*"I came into this world with nothing and I plan to leave it
with nothing,"* remarked a parent.

Unfortunately most people leave this world before they plan to
and what remains are memories and possessions. It is left to the living
to remember them and to dispose of their possessions.

Schools, like other stopping points along life's brief journey, are
places where students "live" while they are acquiring "life skills."
Students pre-kindergarten through high school usually have a combination of the school's and their own possessions to assist them in
acquiring these life skills. When grief comes to visit schools as a result
of a student's untimely death or for some reason being unable to
continue their education, it will be the staff's responsibility to skillfully
and properly deal with their possessions.

Possessions of High School Students

Some people might question that every possession a high school
student has at school is necessary to their education. Some high
school student lockers contain, to say the least, interesting items. But
no matter what is found in high school student lockers or other
places in the building where they keep their possessions, school staff
and crisis response team members must, often times under difficult
circumstances, deal with these possessions.

If the student's possessions are contained in a locker, it is best to clean out that locker when other students are not in school or at least when other students are not in the hallway where the locker is located. Many schools report when they attempt to clean out the locker when other students are around, it often creates a problem and at times becomes another grieving site for some students.

All of the items from the locker should be removed and taken to the administrative offices. A box or a container of some type in which to put the items is better than making several trips between the locker and the administrative offices.

After the possessions have been taken to the office, any items belonging to other students should be identified. Although high school students may be assigned to individual lockers, it is not unusual for them to share lockers. There may be items in the locker that go unclaimed. This is usually because students have forgotten about them or they are too embarrassed to claim them. However, be sure to keep all items that are not claimed by other students or are not returned to the family. These items should not be disposed of until after all possibility exists that they may be needed by authorities as part of any type of investigation. Use discretion in disposing of these items and do not make any of these items available to other students for "keepsakes."

As is usually the case when families are grieving, people reach out to acknowledge the grief and extend their help. Frequently school staff members extend themselves to the family and friends of the student. When appropriate, the personal possessions of the student should be returned to the family. This should be done through direct staff contact with the family and not through an intermediary or the mail. It is this personal contact that creates opportunities to help the family. A residual effect may be the family helping the school or helping other students. But keep in mind that the major intent is to assist the family.

Possessions of Junior High/Middle School Students

In many instances, junior high/middle school students are similar to high school students in that they "reassign" themselves lockers and locker partners. The possessions of these students should, in most instances, be handled in the same manner as high school students. Again, school officials should be cautious of their timing in removing the student's possessions from the locker. Junior high/

middle school adolescents may even have a more emotional reaction than high school students if the locker is cleaned out while students watch. A common mistake made by administrators working with all ages of adolescents is to "invite" students who may have shared the locker to be present when the locker is emptied and ask them to claim their materials and personal items. Claiming personal items should be done in the privacy of an office.

In some instances, particularly with young adolescents, it may be necessary to have them participate in the "disposition" of the student's possessions. This procedure, which is used frequently with elementary students, can be effective in helping some young adolescents understand the finality of a student's death and the fact that they will not be returning to school.

Possessions of Elementary School Students

Books and articles that focus on children and grief often address the developmental stages of children and understanding of death. We know, for example, that at an early age children begin to develop some understanding of death. But we also know that their perceptions are different than those of an adult. There is still some disagreement regarding the specific age at which children gain a mature understanding of death. Studies do show that factors such as personality, sociological and cultural environments, prior experiences with death and death issues, and a number of other factors influence children's perception of death (Wolfelt, 1983).

Keeping in mind that elementary school students are at varying levels of understanding regarding death and death issues, it is important to assist these children in understanding the finality of death, especially when one of their classmates dies. When an elementary school student dies, the proper handling of his or her possessions is important.

Elementary school students may have lockers, but usually they keep their school and some personal belongings in their school desk. It is important that the teacher(s) not clean out the dead student's desk or remove the student's things prior to when the survivors, in this case the classmates, return to school. With the assistance of one or two members of the crisis response team, the classroom teacher should help the students in the classroom deal with the possessions of the student.

This process begins after the students in the classroom have had an opportunity to talk about the death of their classmate and share their feelings, concerns, and stories about death experiences in their own lives (frequently younger students want to talk about the death of pets). This sharing time is usually done in small groups. Some students will not want or have anything to share. A few students may need individual assistance and may need to be helped in a setting other than the classroom, i.e., crisis room.

After the students have had time to process what has happened, some students, again depending on their age, may want to draw pictures or write something about the dead student. Other students may not have an interest in doing any type of activity. Using the best judgment of the classroom teacher and the crisis team members who are in the classroom, a decision should be made as to when the most appropriate time would be to deal with the dead student's possessions.

At the appropriate time, students should be encouraged to become involved in deciding what to do with the possessions in the student's desk. Don't forget the other items in the classroom that may belong to the student or have his or her name on them, i.e., art work, stories or poems that are being displayed in the room, name tags or lists with names of students participating in certain types of groups, or animals or plants that the student may have brought to school.

Experience has shown that many of the students in the classroom will want to be involved in deciding what to do with the student's possessions. These decisions range from deciding what needs to be collected and given to the student's parents, what belongs to the school and needs to be returned, and what to do with various personal items around the room and possibly in the school hallway. Don't be surprised if some students what to claim some of the personal items for their own.

Most students are usually quite involved during this activity. There may be some tears on the part of adults as well as students, but don't be surprised to hear some laughter and see some smiles.

Since many elementary classrooms celebrate student birthdays, eventually the students will, if the birthday has not already occurred, discuss the dead student's birthday and whether the class should celebrate it. This, or any classroom event that gives students the opportunity to celebrate their lives, may be the single most important feature of this activity.

Throughout this activity the students in the classroom have had, through their management of the dead student's possessions, an opportunity to begin to say good-bye to their fellow classmate. For some students, this activity will have helped them realize their classmate is dead and will not be coming back to school. But don't overlook the importance of giving the students in the classroom the opportunity to remember their fellow student during certain times throughout the remainder of the school year through the celebration of birthdays and other events.

Students, as well as some adults who have experienced loss through death, frequently recount their observation that a short time after the death it seemed like the person's name was not mentioned. Some even recall it was almost as if the dead person never existed. Our message to students, as we take advantage of the "opportunity" that a crisis presents is: it is all right to remember and to celebrate someone's life even after that person has died. For some students, the preceding activity will begin a process that hopefully will carry over into adulthood.

Meeting with the Student's Family

Determining the appropriate time to meet with the family to offer help, share information, and give them the possessions of their student is an individual matter and should be done in the most compassionate way possible in order to turn an uncomfortable time into one that may provide comfort. Some suggestions for this meeting are:

1. An administrator or teacher who knew the student should accompany a member(s) of the crisis team.

2. The site of the meeting should be determined by the family, i.e., the home, the school.

3. If one of the purposes of the meeting is to discuss the funeral time (see Chapter 13), the meeting should be scheduled prior to when the family begins to make arrangements with a mortuary.

4. Take your cue from the family as to the length of the meeting.

5. If necessary, schedule an additional time to meet with the family. They may want school staff to keep them up to date on how students and staff are reacting and may also want school staff to deliver cards, art work, and poems students are writing to the family.

6. Don't avoid having the meeting with the family. It is natural to feel somewhat uncomfortable. Relax and remember you are doing the best you can. That is all anyone can expect.

The possessions of the student, though they may be cumbersome to deal with, are a key link in the delivery of a complete and successful response to a school crisis, so take advantage of the opportunities presented.

After Thoughts

Dealing with the students possessions can be uncomfortable, and it may even be upsetting to people assigned to the task. All possessions the student has at school, not belonging to the school or other students, should be returned to the family. I was reminded of this "up close and personal" by a workshop participant. During a break in the workshop, I was approached by a member of the audience who described a personal tragedy and the loss of one of their sons in a traffic accident. This individual impressed the need for all personal items of a deceased student to be returned to the student's family.

School administrators and crisis team members also need to develop appropriate plans for dealing with the possessions of staff in the event of a staff member's death. Some schools have reported that students have wanted to have some of their teacher's possessions and, in a few instances, have stolen the teacher's personal possessions after learning of the teacher's death.

Whoever the school person or persons assigned the task of dealing with the possessions of students or staff, they need to be mindful of the possible need for law enforcement officials to view or review the possessions before they are removed from the school setting. Some crisis response protocols require law enforcement notification prior to removing a deceased individuals possessions from their storage site in the school.

Chapter 11

The Management of Follow-up

"I'm really worried about Kelly. She is taking this so hard."
"Ericka lost her mother last summer and now her boyfriend has been killed. Her dad will really have his hands full now." "These kids have had five of their classmates die in the past two years. Someone told me that many of them are wondering who will be next."

Follow-up. The word itself is interesting. Does it mean to follow-though or to follow-along, to keep track of or keep an eye on, to watch or to observe, to check on or to check off? Is it an action word or is it passive? And, if you can figure out what it is, who is responsible for doing it?

Crisis response teams in schools are typically forty-eight to seventy-two hour events. This means crisis response teams are not normally involved directly in a school or schools for more than two or three days after a tragedy occurs. By this time, most of the student and staff issues have been addressed and the crisis team disperses and team members return to their "real" jobs.

So, who does the follow-up/follow-through/checking off/checking on school staff, students, and parents regarding all of the issues and concerns that have arisen in connection with the tragedy? Let's begin by discussing who doesn't do it.

Staff on school crisis response teams, if they are to maintain their non-anxious presence, their energy to respond again, and their long term mental health, need to have closure to crisis events. They are trained to provide an early, immediate, and effective intervention and are not or should not be expected to provide long term assistance to school staff, students, and parents. They also have other duties in the school district and need to return to their school district and other assignments at the earliest appropriate time.

Frequently crisis response teams provide the school administrative/counseling team with information on various school staff, students, and parents/families. This information may be broken down by varying levels of risk regarding staff, students, and home situations or circumstances. The information could pertain to side issues that arose during the response. All of the information the crisis team deems useful to school staff, students, and families should be passed along from the crisis team to appropriate administrators, counselors, and other staff. If a portion of this information is sensitive or confidential, it should be treated as such.

Five Organizational Tips

Even though a crisis response team may not be directly involved in the majority of the follow-up efforts, the team should assist the school by providing an organizational structure for the follow-up process.

1. Provide an alphabetized listing of all students who came in contact with the crisis team. Pertinent information such as parent contacts should be shown on the listing.

2. The crisis team leader should chair the follow-up meeting.

3. The crisis team should meet prior to the follow-up meeting to organize, screen and streamline the information the team needs to share.

4. Crisis team members should be prepared to suggest the type(s) of follow-up they deem appropriate for individual students or staff.

5. The crisis response team leader should schedule "a follow-up meeting to the follow-up meeting." The purpose of this meeting should be to share information that will assist the crisis response team in future responses and assist them in refining follow-up/follow-through techniques.

Referral Resources

Many of the students and staff who need follow-up work after a crisis may be referred to school resources. These resources might include school counselors, school psychologists, school social workers, and school nurses. Depending on the size of the school district, these referral resources may be the same or many of the same staff who have responded to the crisis event.

In addition to school resources, crisis teams may have the option of using community, county-wide, or statewide referral resources. This might include mental health agencies, hospitals, and private mental health practitioners. In some school districts, crisis teams may have access to private referral resources for consultation purposes as well as using these resources to assist students, families, and staff.

In making referrals, crisis team members and/or staff responsible for follow-up should:

1. Use the school's resources whenever possible.
2. Give students and staff a variety of referral options.
3. Have the person(s) responsible for follow-up determine if a referral is necessary. Whenever possible, the person(s) doing the follow-up should make the actual referral.
4. Involve parents in the referral process.

Case Managers

Assigning a staff person to manage follow-up procedures can be very effective. These "case managers" can be any staff person, certified or classified. The case manager's responsibility is to maintain communication with the student(s) and staff assigned to them. For low risk students this may only require an occasional contact with the students and their parents or teachers. For medium and high risk students more frequent contact is needed, particularly in the days, and in some cases weeks, immediately after the event.

Procedures should be in place for case managers to report any concerns they have about the students and/or staff assigned to them for follow-up. If possible, case managers should have an individual or small group available for consultation. This resource should be available to the case managers on a twenty-four hour basis.

Managing the Overload

In some school districts, the staff on the crisis response team who respond to the crisis event will be the same staff responsible for the follow-up process. Although this may be manageable, it is far from ideal.

Crisis team members who are assigned follow-up responsibilities should:

1. Be certain they have been involved in a thorough debriefing of the crisis event.
2. Have been involved in a Critical Incident Stress Debriefing/Defusing prior to being assigned follow-up duties. (See Chapter 15)
3. Have the opportunity, if they have been significantly effected by the event, to decline to participate in the follow-up process.
4. Be permitted to team with another case manager to do follow-up.
5. Be relieved of follow-up responsibilities if the crisis team is called for another crisis event within six weeks to two months of the last event.

Moving On

Students and adults should be encouraged to move through the grief process at their own pace. If this is allowed, it will help those still impacted by the crisis event and/or those grieving personal issues that resurfaced during the crisis.

Even though the staff assigned follow-up tasks need to allow people to move at their own pace with grief issues, they need to realize this may make the follow-up process more difficult and lengthy. Staff assigned as case managers need to continue to monitor those assigned for follow-up for as long as the "moving on" process requires.

After Thoughts

Well trained and organized school crisis response teams can make a difference in the lives of many people during times of school tragedies. Done properly, school crisis response is an effective, and now proven, tool to assist students and staff with loss issues. But, then the crisis moment ends and life goes on. What about the students and staff who have continuing issues related to the crisis event? What does a crisis team do for them over a prolonged period of time?

The concept of doing long term follow-up with some students and staff after a crisis event appears to look good on paper. But, does it work in reality? Let's face it, the majority of school crisis response teams are staffed by individuals who work for the school district in various capacities. I have yet to meet individuals from a school district's crisis response who devote full-time, or even a major portion of their time, to responding to significant crisis events having the potential to greatly impact student learning. These people, perhaps like you, have full-time jobs, *plus* they have accepted the responsibility of helping during difficult and stressful events. Where are these people going to find the time to do long-term follow-up for those having protracted reactions to particular events?

School crisis teams might best limit their formal follow-up procedures to activity planning for the anniversary dates of crisis events and not attempt to do long-term follow-up in formal and organized ways. This does not mean the long-term needs of some students or staff should be ignored. It does mean that given the real life factors of time and availability of organized crisis team efforts, long-term follow-up might be best left to others.

Chapter 12

The Letter

Communication is a key ingredient in life. Our ability to effectively translate our thoughts and ideas to others is essential if we want success in our careers and private lives. Most school districts pride themselves on their ability to successfully communicate with students, parents, and the community. This chapter focuses on using a letter to effectively communicate with parents after a school tragedy.

Although communication via the media may be appropriate in sharing brief items of information with parents and the community, one of the most effective ways to communicate directly with parents is in writing, i.e., a letter. Depending on the age of the students, this letter is given to them to take home or is sent home by mail. (For some strange reason, we have convinced adolescents that any letter the school gives them to take home to their parent(s) contains trouble. You usually can send the letter home with elementary students, but you may have to mail it to the homes of middle/junior high and high school students.)

Basically, the letter that is sent home to the parent(s) is a four-part letter. Part 1 tells the parent(s) what has happened. Part 2 explains what the school is doing about it. Part 3 gives the parent(s) information that will help them assist their student(s) at home, and part 4 informs the parent(s) about any scheduled meetings and the funeral.

The Letter, Part 1

The first paragraph of the letter informs the parent(s) about the crisis event. Avoid lengthy details or specific information that might not be public knowledge. Do not include unverified information or information that is subject to change. Terms like murdered, committed suicide, was strangled, and was decapitated should be avoided. If the letter is being written regarding a student/staff death, use appropriate terms such as died or killed. Avoid euphemisms like "passed away," "expired," "went to their great reward," "lost," and "went to sleep."

The Letter, Part 2

Part 2 of the letter should tell the parents what the school district is doing about the crisis event. If possible, avoid the use of comments like, "a team of counselors and psychologists are working with students" or "members of the clergy are talking with students." Terms like, "members of the school district's response team" or "the school district's crisis response team" are acceptable terms to the parents and the community. "Trained school district staff members" or "district staff trained to help student/staff" are additional ways of explaining who is working with the students and staff. If you don't mention this information in the letter, parents may become suspicious of what the school district is trying to do or is doing to their students. Depending on the school system, i.e., private vs. public, some of these terms may be more acceptable than others.

The Letter, Part 3

This portion of the letter explains why you are sending information home and offers parents suggestions on helping their students. This part of the letter is the school's way of telling the parents that they need to become involved in helping their students and that the school and the home need to work together. You can also give the parents a phone number to call if they want additional help. Frequently, when parents call, this is the first indication the school has that a particular student is having difficulty.

The Letter, Part 4

The final part of the letter gives the parents information about the funeral and, depending on the crisis situation, other information that the parents may need. The parents should, if possible, be informed via the letter of the funeral arrangements. If that information is not available, a statement like, "funeral arrangements are pending" or "check the local newspaper for information regarding the funeral," could be used. It is important this portion of the letter convey to the parents that if their student is going to attend the funeral, a parent must send a note to school excusing the student. Not only does this put the parents in charge of whether their student attends the funeral, but it also indirectly informs the parents that school will not be dismissed. This portion of the letter should also suggest to the parents that if their student plans to attend the funeral, a parent should also attend.

Things to Remember About the Letter

1. The letter is written by a person or persons on the crisis team and submitted to the principal for editing/approval. After the principal and the crisis team leader have agreed to the contents of the letter, it should be typed on paper containing the school's letterhead. Always proofread the letter after it has been typed.

2. The principal *always* signs the letter. If the principal is not available to sign the letter, i.e., is out of town, *the principal still signs the letter.* With prior approval from the principal, the school secretary could use a signature stamp or sign the principal's name. Because of the importance of the letter containing the principal's signature, the crisis team should work with all administrators in the school district to assure them of the team's competence in writing this type of letter. One method of doing this is to provide administrators with sample letters. Do this before any crisis event.

3. The letter should be written in a way the lay public will understand. Do not use jargon and terms specific to the educational profession. If the parents can't understand the letter or the letter is written in a way that can be misinterpreted, the school and/or the crisis team may have created another crisis.

4. Keep in mind that the letter may have a wider audience than just the parents of the school, i.e., the board of education could receive a copy, it might be printed in the local newspaper, portions of it may be read on radio or television.

5. Create a new letter for each crisis situation. Do not write a generic letter covering all crisis events that simply requires blanks to be filled in for each specific event. Do not edit letters used for previous crisis events to try to make them fit the current event.

6. Keep in mind this letter, for the majority of the parents, will be the only communication they receive from the school. Therefore, it is an important document and is a vital part of the total crisis response plan.

Facts vs. Rumors

During the early stages of crisis events, accurate information is often difficult to acquire. One of the problems in writing the letter is distinguishing between facts and rumors and determining which sources of information are the most reliable.

For example, one school district, after receiving assurance from the police that an elementary student was legally in the crosswalk before he was struck and killed by the driver of a car, sent a letter to parents which included this information. Twenty-four hours later, the police, after further investigation, determined the elementary student was not legally in the crosswalk.

In another crisis, a letter was sent home to parents announcing the death of a student. Shortly after the letter was given to students to take home, officials learned the hospitalized student was still alive.

How do you know the information you have is factual? The crisis team should confirm the information with as many sources as possible. However, if the team waits until a crisis event to establish contact and attempts to build a relationship with information sources, i.e., police, fire, hospital, local or state officials, it may be difficult to get much information. These sources should be "cultivated" prior to any crisis event.

Writing for Different Audiences

"Write the letter so the people in the brown house across the street can understand what happened and what we are doing about it," commented a crisis team leader as he looked out of a window in the school. "They are our customers and we need to communicate effectively with them."

As noted earlier, the letter may have different audiences such as students, staff, parents, community, and the media. All of these audiences should be considered as the letter is drafted. But the main audience is the parents of the students who attend the school where the tragedy occurred. It is vitally important they have a general understanding of what has occurred and are aware of the resources available to their students. It is important to focus the letter on this audience. Depending on the circumstances, it may be equally important to consider the diversity of other audiences who may also have an interest in the contents of the letter.

The Letter as a Teaching Tool

Sometimes opportunities present themselves in strange and, as the Chinese definition of crisis, says, "dangerous" ways. The tragedy of a school crisis will present many positive opportunities—one of which is the chance to communicate with the public while you have their full and undivided attention.

It is at this time the letter can be a useful tool in not only providing information to parents and assisting them; but, it also demonstrates another area of expertise the school district has available for students and families. Don't underestimate the importance of the letter in providing this information as well as lowering the level of concern for families and the community at large.

After Thoughts

As a result of helping school districts deal with the deaths of over 2,600 students and staff, my after thoughts regarding "The Letter" are short and to the point—send it. I know of no other activity in a school district's crisis response arsenal that is more effective and has as much positive impact as sending a letter to parents during a school crisis event.

School crisis teams and school administrators should also consider drafting and sending a letter home, not only during local crisis situations, but during tragedies that impact a state or the nation. Most parents welcome opportunities to learn how to better communicate with their students. Sometimes those learning opportunities may come during difficult and stress filled times.

Chapter 13

The Funeral

The Power of Funerals

The beginnings of this chapter were being written at the same hour as a funeral was being conducted for a father and his son. Their plane crashed and brought their planned fishing trip to a sudden and fatal conclusion. Several crisis response team members attended the funeral and witnessed a variety of expressions of sadness and grief. And, in the faces and through the comments of the team members who attended the funeral, one could see and hear the influence the funeral had on each of them as they observed a wife/mother and her two surviving children grieving the death of a husband/son/father/ brother. A number of lives, including those of some of the crisis team members, had been forever changed.

Funerals, concluding rituals, or whatever name they are called, have been or will probably be significant experiences in the lives of most people. These are times when families usually share their mourning with friends and sometimes the general public. Funerals are one of several ways for mourners to say good-bye to someone who has died. Whatever your likes and dislikes, opinions or feelings about funerals, they are very much a part of real life.

Funerals can be powerful. They can aid the grief process and provide comfort. They can help with the reconciliation that a loved one, close friend, or acquaintance has died. They can make the dead person's life seem greater than it actually was. They can trigger deep emotions and even cause people to want to give up their lives so they can "join" the person who has died. Funerals can evoke relief, anxiety, anger, emptiness, joy, and many other feelings.

Funerals for young people can be extremely powerful. For the first time, many young survivors realize they are not immortal. Depending on the age of the students who are in attendance, the funeral may be the first time some young people come to the realization their friend is not going to come back.

Another factor which influences the power of funerals is whether there is an open or closed casket. Young people frequently comment if the casket is closed, it is much more difficult for them to associate with the fact their friend is inside the casket. At times they don't feel they had an opportunity to say good-bye.

However, if the casket is open, students and other young friends may say good-bye in ways that may not be acceptable to adults. For example, a funeral director in a western state recalled when students who were attending a funeral literally took the student's body out of the casket and began holding and hugging it. The funeral director related most of the adults who were attending the funeral were quite shocked at the proceedings, yet the students seemed comfortable with what was transpiring.

Sometimes students may not attend the funeral, but they may attend a "viewing" of the body/casket. At a viewing the casket may be open or closed. Viewings can also be powerful experiences and may evoke responses similar to what may occur at the funeral. Frequently, viewings are not structured and adult supervision may be limited so students might have less support than they do at the funeral.

No matter what the setting for the concluding ritual, many of the students who attend a viewing or the funeral may be there out of curiosity. Most students will have seen dead people on television, but they may never have actually seen a dead body. The student's reactions to seeing the body may vary. Many adults report vivid memories of their first experiences with death issues and seeing a dead person.

Determining Who Should Attend the Funeral of Elementary Students

Parents of elementary students often wonder if their child should attend the funeral and frequently will follow the lead of school staff in making this decision. They often have concerns about the funeral's effect on their child and can be ambivalent about making a decision. Depending on the ages of the elementary students and their developmental level, parents are sometimes concerned about the students concept of death and they express fears of their child having sleep difficulties, unnecessary worries, or express concerns about religious overtones.

Although it may be appropriate for school personnel to dialogue with parents regarding whether their child should attend the funeral, the final decision should be the parents'. The school's position should be that if the child is going to attend the funeral, a parent or another significant adult should accompany the child.

There may be some parents who will not allow their children to attend the funeral. In some instances, these can be children who were close friends or playmates of the dead student. School staff or crisis team members may need to design alternatives for these students that will allow them to say good-bye to their friend. This may be done in small group or one-on-one sessions. At some point, students who did or did not attend the funeral may choose to be in a grief group. Parents should be notified of this desire and information regarding a grief curriculum should be shared with the parents.

Middle School/Junior High School Students

Young adolescents, although they may have trouble accepting the death of a friend or loved one, are beginning to see death as inevitable and they usually have a realistic perception of death. Their desire to attend the funeral may be more influenced by their peers than their parents. If they do attend the funeral, they often prefer to sit with friends rather than adults.

These young students are in the beginning stages of wanting more independence, but the majority of them are very much in need of a parent or adult presence at the funeral. Although these students are seeking independence and are becoming more mobile, they must still rely on adults for most of their transportation needs. Parents or other adults who are transporting young adolescents should attend the funeral and not just "drop them off." Because of their susceptibility to major mood swings and their need for adult support, young teenagers should be closely monitored by supportive adults before, during, and after the funeral.

High School Students

Of the three groups of school age students who may attend the funeral, high school students will be the most independent and can be the most difficult. Some high school students will need, with the help of an adult, to explore their feelings about attending the funeral. Most will make their decision based on their relationship with the dead student and/or peer pressure. Most frequently high school students are not accompanied at the funeral by parents or other adults. Because of their mobility, they may also attend the internment after the funeral.

Some high school students may attend the funeral because of their association with a particular group of students, i.e., musical, athletes. Some of these students may not know the dead student well, but may still be involved in the funeral.

As is true with all ages of students, parent and adult attendance and support at the funeral is advisable. Crisis team members should be particularly alert for high school students who appear to be "having problems" at the funeral and should insure immediate fol-low-up occurs with those students and their families.

School Staff

The issue of which staff members attend a funeral needs to be addressed if a funeral is held during school hours. This can be a difficult issue with student funerals and a significant issue with current or former staff member's funerals.

Some school districts have policies that govern staff attendance at funerals. Experience has demonstrated that regardless of the school policies, school officials should assess the need for particular staff to attend the funeral and, if necessary, deviate from the policies.

Care should be taken not to place staff in a position where they feel as if they are being required to attend the funeral. Some staff members will, for personal and other reasons, wish not to attend. Conversely, there will be some staff members who do not want to attend the funeral, but may need to do so. Crisis team members should use their skill in assessing these situations and make appropriate recommendations to administrators and individual staff members.

Influencing the Funeral Time and Place

It should be obvious some of the funeral issues that frequently confront school personnel (i.e., who should attend the funeral, do students need an excuse to attend, should teachers or other staff accompany students to the funeral, should school be dismissed for the funeral), may not become issues if the funeral is conducted outside school time. Sometimes these and other issues can create additional crises for the school. Therefore, it is appropriate for crisis teams to try to influence the time of the funeral.

Most funeral times are determined by the schedules of facilities (church, mortuary) or the schedules of people (clergy, family, and relatives). Or, in some communities, funerals are held at certain times, i.e., 10:00 a.m. or 2:00 p.m., because of tradition. Seldom is the schedule of the school taken into consideration. This issue may even be more complex if the family requests the funeral be held at the school.

Many families do not indicate a funeral time preference but respond to the suggestions of funeral directors and clergy. Unless there is a significant scheduling problem, such as a relative arriving at a specific time and having to return within a short period of time, many families indicate they would have been receptive to suggestions from school officials regarding the time the funeral could be conducted.

Frequently, school staff members contact families who are grieving the death of a student or staff member. This contact is usually to extend sympathy; deliver cards, flowers, and food; or to ask how they may be of assistance to the family. It is during such times, especially if it is shortly after the death, it may be appropriate to visit with the family about the funeral plans. Times and locations may be suggested along with the rationale for having the funeral after school hours and in a location that can accommodate staff and students wishing to attend.

Another way school officials and crisis teams can influence the time and place of funerals is to plan meetings with local clergy and funeral directors. These meetings need to be held prior to a tragic event. Most schools who have held these meetings report excellent cooperation from both of these groups. They have also reported both groups indicated they were never aware that funeral times (during school hours, and locations, i.e., school gyms) were issues that effected schools.

Six Duties for Crisis Team Members Attending the Funeral

Members of the crisis response team should attend the funeral. Depending on the situation, this may mean the entire team or some members from the team. Whichever the circumstance, those members of the team who do attend the funeral have specific duties:

1. **Know what the students have experienced.** It is imperative some members of the crisis team attend the funeral so they are aware of what transpired and can have some understanding of what the student and staff attending the funeral have experienced.

2. **Observe reactions of students and staff.** Often times students or staff members will exhibit different behaviors at the funeral than they may have exhibited at school. Care should be taken to record those behaviors for the purpose of follow-up. If the method for recording behaviors is observation and memory, names of students and staff who may have revealed certain behaviors, i.e., first public display of tears, exiting prior to the end of the funeral, hysteria, should be logged as soon as possible after the funeral. The crisis response team should establish procedures for handling this type of information and the appropriate follow-up.

3. **Offer assistance where needed.** At a funeral for a kindergarten student who was accidentally shot when his fourth grade brother handed him a loaded revolver, the fourth grade brother was observed standing by the casket holding and stroking his dead brother's hand and repeating, "I'm sorry, I'm sorry...." The boy's family was too distraught to help the fourth grader and a crisis team member who was attending the funeral put her arms around the young boy and held him as he cried softly. At times, members of the family, students, staff, or parents may need the assistance of a member of the crisis team to help with certain situations that arise. Crisis team members need to be proactive in reaching out at the funeral to those who may need their assistance.

4. **Take care of yourself.** Some members of the crisis response team, even though they may not have previously known the dead student, may need to attend the funeral for personal reasons. It is important these individuals speak out regarding their desire to attend the funeral and, depending on the circumstance, they not be assigned response team duties at the funeral.

5. **Assess student risk.** Depending on the general reaction of students, the extent of parent/adult attendance and support, and the public comments of the minister or others who speak, the funeral may cause some students to be at risk. In the case of funerals for students who have committed suicide, this level of risk may increase. One crisis team noted that the type of music played at the funeral of a young adolescent who hung herself, caused increased student emotion and, in their opinion, lead to the suicide of another student two days after the funeral. Crisis team members need to be alert to signs of at risk behaviors on the part of students and respond appropriately. Such signs might include: undue emotion or lack of it; comments about joining the deceased or going to say good-bye; unusual behavior changes at school or home; recent or increased fascination with death; or talk about suicide and access to firearms.

6. **Access to the student's family and parents of other students.** Even though the crisis team may have visited with the student's family and worked with parents of other students through discussions at school or over the phone, the funeral provides a unique opportunity for some crisis team members to connect with these two groups. The funeral setting frequently encourages one-on-one and small group conversations that might be beneficial to crisis team members as well as others.

Responding After the Funeral

"You should have seen the party we had out at Lisa's grave the night after the funeral. It was like she was there. Some people said they talked to her."—High school senior.

"Every day I find notes and poems from Sam's friends. And there are always fresh flowers on the grave."—Mother who's son was killed in a car accident.

"I keep hoping he will come back to school and we can play together at recess."—First grade student's comment after his friend's funeral.

"After the funeral, we all got together at Amy's house. Although there were some funny things, most of the time we just watched movies and cried. It's hard to believe that Matt is gone forever."— middle school student.

Depending on the circumstances, the funeral may not signal the end of the crisis event nor conclude the work of the crisis response team. Though the school climate tends to revert to the routine, some students will be effected for varying lengths of time. Although the crisis team should not become involved in long term follow-up with students, the team may need to be involved in an organized response that could last up to a week after the funeral.

Consideration should be given to opening the school immediately after the funeral/memorial service. This is especially significant if the crisis event involved adolescents. It may be necessary to keep the school open for several hours to accommodate those students and families who attend the internment or other post-funeral events.

Having the school open after the funeral assists in providing closure to the event and gives students the opportunity to relate their feelings about the funeral and other issues of concern to them. This is usually a time when some students, although still grieving, feel a sense of relief. Their focus is more toward the future and some students have an aura of optimism. This provides an excellent opportunity to work with students in a more positive environment than may have existed prior to the funeral.

Warning Signs

Even though the school's response to the crisis has been successful and the response of students and staff went as predicted, the activities surrounding the funeral may provide clues to other problem issues related to the crisis event. Some warning signs to be aware of are:

1. Large numbers of students having difficulty in resolving their grief.
2. The majority of the students not returning to the routine of the school day.
3. A significant number of students insisting the school establish a memorial for the student on school property.
4. There are reports of students exhibiting risk behaviors, i.e., use of alcohol and other drugs, suicide attempts.
5. Students needing support are not receiving it outside the school setting.
6. School officials are unsure of how to manage difficult students or situations and no planning has been done to assure appropriate responses.

7. The community is not in support of the school and is attempting to intervene.

8. The media continues to highlight the crisis.

These warning signs are just that—warning signs. School crisis response teams should be prepared to respond to any of these or other situations and may need to extend beyond the normal time commitment for a crisis response. Even though some of the warning signs are not within the school's control, plans need to be made to attempt to bring the crisis situation to closure. Part of this planning would be outlining appropriate follow-up procedures and revising the school district's crisis response plan to minimize these situations the next time grief visits the school.

After Thoughts

If I never attend the funeral of another student as long as I live, that would be fine. Many things stand out from all those difficult and sad student funerals, but one that sticks most in my mind is the numbers of middle and particularly high school age students who attend funerals unaccompanied by an adult. Often times these students seem adrift in these settings. But, usually there are some school staff members present at these funerals who do an appropriate and effective job of assisting these students.

It is at viewings where I see students often struggle, and often without the assistance of an adult. School crisis response teams may wish to help prepare students for these visitation experiences. For those students who plan on attending a visitation or funeral, it would be beneficial for you to cover informally what students might expect and to review proper etiquette. Teachers can be given information and encouraged to discuss the following points with their students.

- It is appropriate to dress up if the student is planning to attend either the visitation or the funeral.

- Visitation is meant to provide a time to support family members and honor the person who has died.

- Generally, visits are brief, but some families will plan a formal prayer service during the visitation.

- At the visitation, the casket will be present and may be open. It is customary to view the casket and/or body. Some families may have a "kneeler" so individuals may offer a short prayer.

- The body may not look like the person you remember. Some people may gently kiss or touch the body.

- It is okay to view the casket in small groups, and it is okay to talk quietly. However, it is best not to congregate around the casket. Move away to allow others the opportunity to pay their respects.

- Some people like to leave flowers or other remembrances. If there is no table, it is best to leave them with the family. It is not appropriate to place remembrances inside the casket.

- It is appropriate to greet family members and to express your sorrow. A simple statement such as, "I am sorry for your loss" will let the family know that you care.

- Funeral services vary according to the culture and religious preferences of the family. It is respectful to follow the religious customs. Arrive at the funeral site early to allow time to sign a guest book and be seated.

- Attendance at the cemetery (internment) is optional, but it is important to leave soon after the services to give the family a time of privacy.

Chapter 14

The Related Issues

There is probably a quote somewhere that says, "Nothing is as simple as it may appear." If there isn't, there is now! This quote is frequently true when it comes to the effective management of a school crisis. Anything and everything can and sometimes does happen. This chapter provides information on managing side issues that may occur during a response to a school tragedy.

Memorial Paradigms

People memorialize people. The rich and the not so rich and famous will be memorialized, some during their life times and some after they have died. These memorials may range from adulation to stones with dates and names, photographs, and creative works.

Memorials and the need to remember people are frequent issues that arise during or shortly after a school's response to a student or staff member's death. Requests for some type of remembrances may come from a variety of sources including students, staff, and the community. These requests usually are acts of kindness and may result from the "emotion of the moment." Although well intended, these initiatives are often not well thought out and any long-term implications for the school and its students or staff usually have not been considered.

A central question regarding memorials concerns whether it is the school's responsibility to memorialize people after they have died or whether this is the responsibility of the family and friends of the deceased. The answer to this question may be different depending on previous practices of the school or various school/community memorial paradigms.

If, for example, the practice in a school or community has been to commemorate students and staff who have died by dedicating a plaque, picture, monument, yearbook, tree, retired athletic uniform, or holding a memorial service during school hours, then this memorial paradigm may have continuing support. Conversely, if the school or community has considered these types of remembrances as not being the responsibility or role of the school or view them as potentially harmful, these practices may not exist.

School administrators, with the help of crisis response team members, should establish guidelines for students, staff, and the community regarding school memorials. If at all possible, these guidelines should be established prior to a crisis event. In some communities, boards of education have established policies concerning memorials. Examples of these policies are:

The board of education reserves the right to accept or reject any and all memorials donated or purchased in memory of a student or staff member. Furthermore, the board of education reserves the right to cause all memorials currently on school properties to be discontinued.

OR

Memorials that contain or would cause any of the following to occur may be rejected by the board of education.

1. Memorials that contain the name and/or picture of the deceased.
2. Memorials that may alter the routine of a regular school instructional day.
3. Memorials that require the retirement or discontinued use of school property.
4. Memorials that require the altering of school property or school publications.
5. Memorials that require the altering of school activities or the school's activities schedule.

6. Memorials that infringe on the separation of church and state.

7. Memorials that require the use of public funds to purchase, develop, or maintain.

Even if school districts have policies and regulations concerning memorials, it is not uncommon for groups of people, i.e., students, staff, and parents to request and even demand that a memorial be established. It is the responsibility of the school staff and crisis team to be accepting of people's need "to remember." Administrators and crisis team members should assist individuals or groups who want memorials and be prepared to offer acceptable memorial options. Some of these options may include:

1. Scholarships established in the names of the students/staff. These are usually acceptable because there is not a permanent display in the school.

2. Furniture, equipment, books, or other instructional materials given to the school should either remain unlabeled or, if donor plaques are acceptable to the school district, they should follow specific guidelines, i.e., given in memory of our beloved son, Carl Jones (not acceptable); given by the Harold and Mary Jones' family (acceptable).

3. Contributions by students/staff to memorials designated by the family, i.e., cancer society, MADD, local charity.

(See the After Thought section of this chapter for more memorial ideas.)

Graduation Ceremonies

Todd, a senior, was killed in a car accident in January. Mike, a classmate, killed himself with a shotgun in March. Todd's friends were pleased with the support they received from the school after his accident. Mike's friends were upset the school did not honor his death. We have already had problems with this issue and I'm really concerned about some type of disruption at our graduation ceremonies. —High School Principal

Sally was killed in a car accident the day before graduation. I don't know whether to postpone graduation or devote a large part of the graduation ceremonies to her memory. —School Superintendent

We want a special seat on the stage with flowers on it, her name read first, and the entire senior class to come forward and receive her diploma in her memory at the graduation ceremonies. —Grieving parents of a high school senior girl killed by a drunk driver

What are we going to do about graduation? What if it's like another funeral with all of the seniors and their relatives in attendance? What if the students become disruptive? What if...? —Concerned Citizen

Graduation from high school is an annual "right of passage" for thousands of seniors. The students, and often their families, have looked forward to this day. It is thought of as a day of celebration, of positive memories, and of thoughts toward the future. Graduation is not perceived to be a day of sadness, unpleasant memories, and hopelessness. Yet, each year many schools and their staffs are challenged to design a graduation ceremony tastefully blending happiness and grief.

Suggestions for designing graduation ceremonies in school districts, where students have died, include:

1. Graduation is a time to recognize the many years of work and achievement of the seniors. If the ceremony plan is to "remember" a student who has died, do this in as short a time as possible and do it at or near the beginning of the graduation ceremony.

2. If the graduation ceremony plan is to award a diploma posthumously, read the name of the deceased student and award the diploma in the same graduation order the student would have received it if present.

3. If the plan is to award a posthumous diploma at graduation to the deceased student's family, arrangements should be made with the family prior to the graduation ceremony.

4. If school tradition is to have students speak at the graduation ceremonies, designated school staff should meet with the students prior to graduation to discuss the content of their presentations. Some schools require students to submit their speeches for approval prior to the graduation ceremony. Even with this precautionary measure, in some instances students change the contents of their speech. Be up front with the students and ask them if they plan to talk about the deceased student. If the speakers plan to devote a portion of their speech to the deceased student, offer suggestions that will hopefully make it a win-win situation for all parties.

5. No matter how well the graduation ceremony is planned, expect the unexpected. It might be beneficial to reconvene the crisis response team and have them review the graduation exercise plans. They may be able to make suggestions to administrators and staff on identifying and handling unexpected situations.

6. Keep the ceremony as positive as possible and in the tradition of previous graduations.

Student/Staff Initiated Responses

Someone once described teaching kindergarten as holding apples down in a tub of water and keeping them from slipping away and popping to the surface. It's almost impossible. The same is true of student and staff issues during a crisis event. Even with the best "lesson plans" for the crisis, usually there are issues that "pop" to the top.

Most schools have policies and regulations regarding student and staff conduct. Frequently these are common sense statements that cover issues such as discipline, safety, absences and extra curricular activities. However, common sense may not always prevail during crisis events. Students and staff may, for whatever reason, initiate ideas and suggestions that may not be in the best short-term or long-term interest of the school. So, what's new about that, one might say. What is new is these student and staff-initiated responses during a crisis occur during extremely emotional and stressful times. The school's appropriate response to them may be critical to the overall success of the crisis response.

Examples of student/staff initiated responses are:

1. Students and/or staff stage a "walkout" because they believe school should be closed in honor of a dead student.

2. Even though it may be against school policy, students/staff want a memorial on display in the school in remembrance of a student.

3. A petition signed by students and/or staff is presented to the administration demanding "whatever."

4. A fund raising drive is initiated to collect money for a memorial. (Some students may not have known or liked the deceased student or may not be able to afford to contribute. Students have reported that they have feelings of guilt associated with some or all of these money collecting issues.)

5. Friends of a teacher who has died insist that the funeral be held at school during school hours and all students and staff be required to attend.

6. Distraught students takeover the principal's office and threaten or actually take the principal hostage until their demands are met.

These are but a few of the issues that may occur during or after a response to a crisis. All student/staff initiated responses should receive fair and equitable treatment. Most of the problems occur when, because of the extremes of emotions, students and staff perceive the decisions being made disregard people's feelings or are not equitable.

What can school administrators and crisis team members do about student/staff initiated responses? Some suggestions are:

1. Listen carefully to students and staff. Their concerns regarding how the school is managing the response to the crisis event may stem from misunderstanding of what is being done.

2. Crisis teams should anticipate various student and staff responses and have a plan prepared to successfully manage them.

3. If school policies are in place that deal with some of the student and staff issues, stick to the policies. Usually these policies are drafted by the administration and approved by boards of education during less stressful times than those that may occur during a crisis event.

4. Remember students and staff have not had the training and experience crisis team members have had and they may not consider what they are requesting may not be possible.

5. Stick with what you know based on your training, experience, and knowledge of crisis management and dealing with student/staff initiated responses.

Community Involvement

Schools belong to the community and are frequently a reflection of the community. This may or may not be helpful when grief visits a school. There are times when the community (parent community, business community, religious community, taxpayer community, senior citizen community) will want to become involved in assisting the school in its response to the crisis. Although ordinarily experiences with these "various" communities may be positive, there can be overt or covert pressure to respond to the crisis event in ways that may not be in the best interest of the school community. During a crisis, it is vital the school communicate with all of its various communities.

Two of the most effective ways of communicating with your community during a crisis event are: (1) utilize the print, radio, and television media, and (2) the letter sent to parents. Through these avenues a school can advertise its preparedness and briefly describe its response plan.

Another way of communicating with the community is to "tell your story" before a crisis event. Crisis response team members should schedule presentations to service organizations, i.e., Rotary, Lions, Junior League. These presentations give schools the opportunity to communicate with various communities within the community. School PTA's/PTO's offer opportunities to tell your story. Although many of these same parents would receive a letter during a crisis event, this is a chance for parents to hear the school's basic crisis response plans and to ask questions before a crisis occurs. Include school administrators in the presentation. Administrators can share information on specific school policies and procedures that may affect the response to the crisis.

If possible, all school employees, certified and classified should participate in meetings when delicate issues of crisis response are presented and discussed. Because it is always a possibility they may be personally affected by a crisis and because they are frequently asked by members of the greater community about school related issues, it is essential for all school personnel to be knowledgeable about the general school crisis plan.

Who's Going to be Next?

After a series of student suicides, a high school student declared, "Well, so far its been a freshman, a sophomore, and a junior. I bet the next one is a senior!" (Unfortunately, the student was right.)

Among the many challenges that confront school personnel after a tragedy involving the death of a student is the realization by some students that they are going to die. In some instances, students adopt an almost fatalistic approach to life. Some become depressed and others exhibit such "at risk" behaviors as over/under eating, loss of sleep, isolation from friends, and poor academic performance.

Although some of these behaviors may not persist for an extended period of time, crisis teams should suggest age appropriate methods to monitor certain students. In most instances, it should not be the responsibility of the crisis team to do the actual monitoring. Parents should also be encouraged to report concerns they have regarding their students. (See Chapter 11.)

Depending on the school and the community, other related or seemingly unrelated issues may occur during a tragedy. Crisis team members should, in their planning sessions, include opportunities to explore what some of these issues might be and make plans in advance for effective responses. There may be times when these issues may overshadow the initial crisis. The overall success of the entire response will require these issues to be addressed and resolved.

After Thoughts

Of all the "related issues" I have dealt with over my years of helping school districts respond to crisis situations, one of the most difficult issues schools have faced has been the establishment of appropriate ways to remember students and staff after their death.

Earlier in this chapter are some discussions and suggestions on student/staff memorials. An additional memorial option that has some appeal for school districts is the concept of "sunset memorials." These memorials are time limited and, therefore, would not be left in the school building for years and years after the death of a student or staff member.

Some of the guidelines for time-limited student memorials are:

- Memorials will be for students who were enrolled in the school at the time of their death.

- Memorials for students in a school-sponsored yearbook or newspaper will be in accordance with the district policy on student publications and the district curriculum goals for journalism classes. Publication staff will confer with both the school principal and a leader from the district's crisis response team before publishing a student memorial.

- Each school will display, when necessary, a plaque with brass engraving plates to recognize individual students who have died. The plaque will be no larger than twelve inches by fifteen inches. The top of the plaque will be engraved with the words, "In Memory." Individual plates will be engraved with the student's legal name and dates of birth and death. Individual plates will be removed after ten years and offered to the student's parents or guardians. (Some school districts keep the memorial plate up for one year after the students would have completed their education at the school.)

- With the consent of the deceased student's parents or guardians, other student memorials may be established if there is no cost to the school.

School districts also can assist families in identifying appropriate memorials. Some of these memorials may include:

- A memorial scholarship. (It may be helpful if the school district has a foundation with a separate governing body, thus keeping the memorials money in an account separate from school district accounts.)

- Purchase of library books, CD ROMS, school supplies, and equipment, with approval from the principal.

- Monetary funds designated to a particular school activity or department with the approval of the principal.

- Plantings on school grounds (trees, shrubs, perennials). Such plantings may be accompanied by a moveable ground marker no larger than twelve by six inches. The marker will be moved when necessary, as the planting grows and will be removed after ten years and offered to the parents or guardians. (Again, some school districts may choose to shorten the ten years to better coincide with certain school timeframes.)

To address the issue of existing memorials on school property, some school districts have proposed the following:

* Any memorial plaque or name plates in existence at the time these guidelines are adopted, whether in compliance with these guidelines or not, will be removed ten years after the death of the student involved and offered to the parents or guardians. Parents or guardians of deceased students are encouraged to inform the school of any change of address so the school may return plaques, markers, and name plates to them as stipulated.

Chapter 15

The Care of Crisis Teams

Most individuals in "helping professions" are capable of conducting successful interventions. But can they repeatedly respond to the needs of others and continue to intervene successfully? Or do they need assistance in maintaining their response energy and effectiveness? And what about some members of crisis response teams who are not specifically trained in the helping professions, but are repeatedly called upon to assist others especially during times of high stress and crisis?

Following up with Crisis Team Members

The crisis is over. Crisis team members have debriefed the crisis event and have returned to their major responsibilities in the school district, i.e., teaching, counseling, support staff. Plans for an effective follow-up with students and staff needing additional assistance have been implemented. Routine has returned to the school setting. All is well! Or is it?

As one crisis team leader recalled, "I contacted the home of one of my team members at about 6:30 in the morning after a severe car accident. The team member's fifth grade child answered the telephone and indicated that his dad could not come to the phone because he was taking a shower. I requested that the child inform his dad that I was on the phone and the call was urgent. The child replied his parents had a rule about the children in the family bothering them when they were showering. The child also commented to the team leader that his dad told him that if the person from the school calls about people dying, he was to say he was not home."

Not all crisis team members direct their children to say they are not home. However, this may be an example of an individual who has not been offered professional assistance by the school district or has not asked other team members for help. Responding to crisis events is stressful and can have a dramatic impact on the lives of those on the team. School districts should implement practices that assist crisis team members in managing the stress that is inherent in crisis response. Such practices include:

1. Opportunities for team members to meet on a regular basis for continued debriefing, practicing response scenarios, and support for each other.

2. Released time for staff development on issues related to crisis response, i.e., grief issues as they relate to children, adolescents, adults in various cultures, team building and cohesiveness; and managing personal stress.

3. Promoting appropriate recognition for the voluntary efforts of the response team members. (In most school districts, crisis response team members serve without additional benefits such as pay and released time.)

4. Supporting team members in seeking professional help for issues that carry over from a crisis event.

5. Organizing a sufficient number of response teams in the school district to ensure that the same team members do not have to respond to each crisis event, i.e., two teams that respond on an every other month basis, or placing alternates on teams to cover for team members who are unable to respond or are personally effected by the response.

Critical Incident Stress Debriefing

In 1983 Dr. Jeffrey Mitchell wrote a procedure for Critical Incident Stress Debriefing.* It is a structured debriefing procedure that assists individuals in discussing the facts of a crisis event and their thoughts and reactions to the event. This procedure should be incorporated into school crisis team programs.

The personal stress of responding to tragedies in schools can, at times, be similar to the stress of fire fighters, police officers, and other first response personnel. Like first response personnel, school crisis team members can experience psychological issues after a response, i.e., depression, withdrawal, sleep problems, family problems, and recurring stress when they have to respond to similar events.

Critical Incident Stress Debriefing (CISD) can help team members by:

1. Helping them understand their feelings are normal.
2. Generating support from other team members.
3. Giving team members guidelines to help themselves.

It is important CISD is done by trained people that have not responded to the crisis event. Preferably those doing the debriefing should be from another organization. Personnel from Employee Assistance Programs, police and fire departments, and mental health groups are good school resources for Critical Incident Stress Debriefing.

Schools should establish CISD guidelines for crisis team members such as:

1. All team members responding to a student death are required to participate in CISD.
2. All team members responding to a school hostage situation are required to participate in CISD.
3. If an individual team member requests CISD after a team response, all team members who responded must participate.
4. Any costs for Critical Incident Stress Debriefing would be covered by the school district.
5. School personnel with CISD training could offer debriefing to other organizations on a reciprocal basis.
6. CISD for crisis team members should be structured as follows:

    Introduction: Ground rules are set.

    Fact Phase: Team members are encouraged to tell their stories of the crisis event.

    Thought Phase: Team members share their first thoughts upon exposure to the worst part of the crisis.

    Reaction Phase: Feelings and emotional reactions are stated.

    Symptom Phase: The team discusses what has changed in their lives since their response to the crisis, i.e., physical, emotional, and behavioral.

    Teaching Phase: The CISD team provides reassurance that what individuals or the group is experiencing is a normal reaction to a tragedy.

    Re entry Phase: Team members can ask questions and summary statements are made.

*Davis, M. Critical incident stress debriefing: The case for corrections," *Corrections Forum*, October, 1994.

Preparing to Respond Again and Again and Again

"No calls yet this month. Knock on wood!" "It's our team's turn next. Every time the phone rings I wonder if this is it." "If we can just get by without something major this year. I'm still numb from those five deaths last school year." "My mom always said that trouble travels in threes. I wonder when our third crisis will happen."

Even though the school district provides appropriate resources to assist staff in managing the stresses inherent in crisis response, individual team members have to "muster" the physical and mental energy to respond again and again and again. In order to do this successfully, team members should:

1. Avail themselves of the helping services the school district provides.
2. Be open in sharing positive and negative response experiences.
3. Focus on the positive aspects in their lives and the lives of others.
4. See themselves as care receivers as well as care givers.
5. Know "when to say when" and sit out the next response.
6. Treat people kindly, including themselves.
7. Learn how to be appreciated and remember to tell other how much they appreciate them.
8. Reward themselves as often as possible for the wonderful "gifts" they give to others.
9. Remember it takes a special person to do crisis response work.
10. Learn from their work and live each day to the fullest.

After Thoughts

A couple of weeks after conducting a crisis response team training workshop, I received a letter from one of the workshop participants. One portion of that letter really struck home. In that particular letter, the writer related a tragedy that impacted their school district. When traveling to school, six students from their high school were involved in a terrible automobile accident. Three of the students were killed and the other three were critically injured. The letter's author described the issues the crisis team faced during their struggles to help their students, staff, and community deal with this tragedy.

Although others on the team were at times very emotional while the team was responding to the tragedy, this team member did not cry. This person related that it wasn't until I discussed in the workshop the importance of crisis team debriefing and the importance of critical incidence stress debriefing, that this person understood why, several months after a tragedy, some team members found themselves crying uncontrollably over seemingly trivial incidents in their lives.

During times of crisis impacting schools, all too many school districts burn their crisis teams up, burn their crisis team out, and burn their crisis team down. And what happens after all of that, those team members are sent back to their "regular" jobs in the school district to, in some cases, clean up the messes created by their absence.

In general, school crisis response teams are to be commended for the time they take after a school crisis to debrief the effectiveness of their responses. They review the positives of their efforts and make notes of correction on the perceived mistakes they made and plan appropriate adjustments in preparation for their next response. In noting their mistakes, the biggest mistake school crisis teams make is not to gather the together in a timely manner and have team members participate in a CISD experience. School crisis team members and their effectiveness in future responses would be better served by such an experience.

Chapter 16

School Security

School tragedies in Arkansas, Mississippi, Colorado, Oregon, Pennsylvania, Alaska, Kentucky, and other states have brought grief to many schools and forced numerous school districts across America to review their safety and security procedures. Additionally, the Oklahoma City bombing, an increase in workplace violence, and the terrorist attacks on our nation have increased student, staff, parent, and community concern for the safety of individuals and prompted a review of security procedures in all walks of life.

The burden to assure school workplace safety has fallen squarely on the shoulders of school administrators. Although data exists supporting the fact that America's schools are safe, school violence and its coverage by the media has heightened community concerns and forced schools to spend time and other resources to focus efforts toward addressing student safety issues. However, one problem some schools have faced is defining the difference between a *safe* school and a *secure* school.

Most schools in America are *safe*. Playground equipment is designed to prevent, or at least minimize, student injury. Glass in doors is shatterproof. Hallways have nonskid tile, and so forth. However, the focus on school *safety* may not prevent most of the school violence. Instead, perhaps the focus should be on school *security*. School *safety* means students and staff in schools are free from accidental injury. School *security* means students and staff are free from *intentional* harm. In order to assure truly *safe* schools, school administrators and their staffs will have to design and improve more effective school *security* procedures.

The comment is frequently made that there are two types of schools: schools who have had a crisis and schools who haven't had one, but they will someday. Be that as it may, all schools should annually review their school crisis response procedures. One major part of school crisis planning is school security.

Putting Together Your School Security Plan

"Those things don't happen in our community." "We don't have those kinds of students in our schools." "Those things don't happen in schools our size." Most of the school districts who have experienced one or more acts of violence never thought they would be responding to the death of students on their school property.

Most school districts across the nation have investigated, and some have implemented, the use of crisis response plans to prepare for possible tragic incidents. Such incidents can vary from student or staff deaths, acts of violence on school property, community incidents that may disrupt learning in the schools, and national or international events. As schools design or review their school security plans, they may want to consider the following:

- Involving law enforcement and other public safety agencies.
- Conducting a school safety/security audit in each building in the school district.
- Developing school security policies and procedures.
- Identifying key staff responsible for implementing the crisis procedures.
- Developing building-level internal crisis teams.
- Training all staff in responding to a school crisis.

Involving Law Enforcement and Other Public Safety Agencies

"No man is an island." This holds true for school districts as well, particularly during times of tragedy or violence. Schools need to rely on the assistance of various agencies to insure their students and staff will receive the necessary help during and after events that may cause injury or death. Law enforcement, fire protection, and other emergency response personnel may be called on to assist schools during certain events. It is imperative that schools work *in advance* with these agencies to develop effective and appropriate plans for emergencies.

School districts should work with law enforcement to develop appropriate and detailed plans to prevent or respond to possible emergencies. The following should be taken into consideration in working with law enforcement agencies and other emergency response organizations:

- Development of protocols for responding to school emergencies.
- Addressing realistic law enforcement response times to school buildings in the district.
- Knox boxes located near the entrance to all school buildings.
- Incident command sites predetermined at each school site. Consideration should be given to having primary and secondary command sites in each building. One of the incident command sites should be located away from the administrative area and near an outside entrance.
- Maps of schools given to all emergency response agencies.
- Locations of all emergency shutoffs identified. Pictures or a video tape of the locations of the equipment would be helpful.
- Assignment of specific roles of school staff and emergency response personnel during a crisis.
- Roles established *prior* to an event between school/law enforcement and media spokespersons.
- Participation in tabletop scenarios by school/emergency responders.
- Predetermined law enforcement perimeters around school buildings.

Building Security Audit

School administrators should conduct a security audit of each building in the district. Appropriate personnel to conduct security audits could include law enforcement, fire safety experts, architects, and trained security audit staff. Additionally, appropriate school staff should be involved in the school building security audit. Some schools even include students as a part of the security audit, as students sometimes see things adults may overlook or not consider. Security audits should include:

- What security devices are necessary and exist in the school buildings? (Classroom phones, security cameras, metal detectors, etc.)

- Does a clear, up-to-date floor plan of the school exist? Who has it? How is it used?

- Have unsafe areas of the school been identified? What long-range plans have been established to eliminate potential dangers?

- Where do visitors enter the school building? Are they required to have visitor passes? (If visitor passes are used, the pass should indicate the room number or area of the school the visitor has permission to enter. School buildings with multiple floors should have colored passes indicating which floor the person has permission to visit, e.g., yellow floor requires yellow-colored pass, orange floor orange pass, etc. Teachers should be instructed and properly trained to challenge visitors who are in the building with inappropriate passes.)

- How effective is the school's communication system—within the school, with community agencies, with transportation staff?

- Does the school identify all students who could possibly become at risk for dangerous behaviors?

- What are the roles of each school staff person during an emergency?

- How is staff with first-aid training identified to students, other staff, and emergency personnel during an emergency? (Some schools have a building internal crisis team composed of staff having emergency first-aid training. In the event of an emergency, school staff on the internal response team should wear bright colored vests. Emergency responders are alerted to look for these persons during a school emergency.)

- Is there a district-wide common alert code for an intruder in a school building? Is all staff properly trained on the procedures they should follow when they hear the code? Have the school staff and students practiced what to do when they hear the intruder code?

* See Appendix B for detailed security audit procedures.

Developing School Security Policies and Procedures

Usually a crisis increases stress, heightens emotions, and interrupts routine. Preplanning for such events may not decrease stress or lower emotions, but it may provide a roadmap to assist the school district in weathering the crisis event and returning the schools involved to routine as quickly as possible.

School policies can provide a framework for action during times of crisis. Since school policies are usually developed with forethought, insight, discussion, and input, they can guide schools away from chaos, knee-jerk reactions, emotional swings, and increased tension. School districts should put into policy the necessary guidelines to assist their schools and the community during local, national, or international events that may significantly impact student learning and classroom instruction.

School district security procedures should be a part of the district's overall crisis response plan. Twenty-five years ago there were very few school districts that had written specific crisis response plans and procedures for the many types of emergency situations they currently confronted. However, recent years have seen the development of school crisis response plans and even the availability of school crisis plans via the internet and the commercial market. This has been both a plus and a minus. On the positive side, school districts have been able to avail themselves of a multitude of options and build their plans based on the experience and expertise of other school districts. On the negative side, some school districts have adopted plans from other districts without regard for whether the plan fits the needs of their district. (Personal note: The author has critiqued school crisis response plans for hundreds of school districts. On a number of occasions, the author has read "borrowed" school district crisis response plans that have had phone numbers from the districts for which they were originally designed or have contained specific procedures and protocols that would only work in the district originating the plan.)

All staff, certified and classified, should have a copy of the crisis response plan and the procedures they are to follow in the event of a school emergency. However, it should be noted that during times of a crisis event that may significantly impact the school, e.g., shooting, hostage situation, or other violent/emergency event, staff probably will not be able to quickly find the appropriate information in their school's crisis manual if, in fact, they can even find the manual! Therefore, as previously stated, schools should consider developing a one- or two-page information sheet with large font size giving staff a few very specific details as to their responsibilities during a school emergency.

Identify Key Staff Who are Responsible for Implementing the Plan

Who are the best people to respond when a school is confronted with an emergency—administrators, counselors, teachers, secretaries, or others who work in schools? Maybe all of these people could be helpful during an emergency; maybe none of them.

As schools identify and select staff who will assume leadership responsibility during a crisis, they may wish to consider the following:

- Do staff members have children of their own attending the school? During crisis incidents in schools, occasionally staff have abandoned their responsibilities to seek out their own children and attempted to get their children our of harm's way.

- Do some staff members identified to assume leadership roles during a school crisis have advanced life-support training? Emergency personnel response times to school buildings can vary widely depending on the building's location, the nature of the emergency, and the close proximity to organized emergency response. Having a building internal crisis response organized effort as a part of the school overall crisis response plan can be helpful during times of a delayed community-based emergency response.

- Despite their training, will key school staff respond appropriately during a school emergency? During emergency drills, key staff usually respond as they have been trained. Unfortunately, in a real crisis, some schools have discovered that some of those same staff did not live up to their emergency response expectations. Given the fact that even some law enforcement officers may lose a portion of their training efficiencies during times of stress, it is understandable some school staff members may experience un-predictable traumatic reactions. In an attempt to offset this possibility, schools may want to conduct some drills without pre-announcing the drill information to their building internal response staff. This practice may help identify individuals who only react well when they have advance warning and preparation time. Having a drill when administrators or others who may be in a leadership position are not present in the building may also be beneficial.

Developing Building Level Internal Crisis Teams

If there is such a thing as a "standard" in the school crisis response team industry, it may be the use of external and internal school crisis response teams. Many school districts have had external crisis response teams in place for quite some time. External school crisis response teams usually are K-12 in nature and are made up of certified and classified staff who have been trained to do timely interventions across school districts during times of crisis/tragedy. Staff on external school crisis response teams may have specific professional training, but this may not be criteria for serving on a team.

In addition to external crisis teams, numerous school districts have organized building level internal crisis response teams. Criteria for internal response teams may include:

- Staff with emergency life-support training.
- Staff with flexible availability during the regular school day.
- Staff with key building leadership roles.
- Staff with strong leadership skills.
- Staff with strong organizational skills.

Training All Staff in Responding to a School Crisis

When crisis and tragedy impact learning in schools, frequently students turn to school staff members for direction, assistance, consolation, and understanding. Giving direction, assistance, consolation, and understanding may be good attributes, but sometimes they don't come easily during stressful and crisis-filled times.

Comments such as, "I forgot most of my facilitative skills" and "I have never had to deal with that many upset students before" to "I was among those who needed assistance and was in no position to give any assistance to others" are not uncommon after a crisis impacts a school. School staffs should be provided staff development experiences that attempt to prepare them for responding appropriately and successfully during stressful times in both their personal and professional lives. Although school staff members will be required to draw upon previous life experiences during times of school tragedies, it is most likely that a combination of appropriate crisis-response training and life experiences may provide the best possible combination of crisis response strategies during a school crisis.

In order to prepare for a school crisis, school staffs should receive training in, among other things:

- Procedures for a school lockdown.
- How to talk and listen to students during difficult times.
- Procedures for classroom safety.
- Safety and security procedures in the areas of the school for which they are responsible.
- Responding to a variety of crisis and emergency situations.
- Emergency first-aid.
- School evacuation procedures.
- Dealing with suspicious packages in the school.
- Keeping students calm and/or dealing with disruptive students during a crisis.
- Proper communication procedures during a school crisis.
- Responding to threats of or acts of terrorism.
- Appropriate procedures for an impending natural disaster.
- Responding to a chemical or biological attack.
- Dealing with weapons in the classroom or school.
- Crowd control procedures.
- Dealing with personal (self) decontamination/or decontamination of students or other staff.
- Maintaining evidence and the procedures for the chain of evidence.
- Resources available to them after a school crisis.
- Protocols specific to the particular school in which they work.

The Chaos of Crisis

Although school districts develop crisis response plans, those plans don't always reflect preparation for dealing with many of the chaotic situations resulting from emergency events that may impact the students and staff in a school, staff/students in other schools in the district, or other school districts in the community/area. One particular area often overlooked is the issue of a large influx of parents and other adults coming on to school property during a crisis event.

Even though schools may have involved emergency services in the community in the pre-planning stages of response to a crisis or a perceived crisis, those plans don't always work. Even though parents have been informed about school response procedures and are aware of the school's efforts to insure their children's safety, parents may not respond appropriately during times of high anxiety.

School districts and the individual schools in the district need to be certain they are prepared to respond to the needs and fears of large numbers of parents during a school emergency. As a part of their preplanning, school districts should inform parents that in the event of a school evacuation, their students would be transported to an alternate site. This site could be a building within a reasonable distance from the school where students and staff could be safely housed. Some criteria for an alternate school site are:

- The alternate site must be able to house all of the students and staff who have been evacuated.

- The alternate site must be close enough to the primary school site to insure all students and staff could walk or be transported there safely.

- The selection of the alternate site must take into account weather-related issues.

- The alternate site must have communication capabilities.

- The alternate site must be far enough from the primary school site to insure student/staff safety in the event of an explosion at the primary school site.

- The alternate site must be far enough from the primary school site to insure safety of students/staff in the event of chemical-biological attack on the primary school site.

- The alternate site should have activities (games, videos, curriculum materials, etc.) to occupy students until they are released from the alternate site.

- The alternate site should have a security audit conducted prior to its selection as a viable safe building site to house students and staff.

During violent and chaotic times in schools, parents may come to the school site in increased numbers, as compared to a regular school day. They might arrive prior to the first responders. In some communities, citizens and media may monitor emergency response broadcasts. Even though their presence may hamper a swift and appropriate emergency response to a crisis occurring on school property, parents may rush to a school in an effort to be helpful. Parents may actually grab their children and exit the property.

As a part of their crisis response planning, school officials should be prepared to anticipate fire and other safety official's need to bring their equipment onto school property as quickly as possible. If roads and other accesses to school property are blocked by parent vehicles or access to the school is blocked by damage or destruction, first responders may have to drive across playgrounds and other school areas not normally used for such purposes.

In planning school evacuation procedures, school personnel should anticipate the possibility of an unnatural atmosphere on the school grounds. Therefore, it is a good practice for schools to instruct students to exit their building during an emergency drill and walk to a designated place on school property. After students have reached their emergency designated position, teachers may be instructed to take attendance and note the names of absent or missing students. In some school districts, teachers are requested to report the names of missing/absent students to a school official. However, if there are large numbers of adults on school property, school staff may not be able to gain the attention of school officials to report the names of missing or absent students.

School officials should consider the following in planning for school evacuations:

- Students should practice moving a safe distance from the school building.

- Staff should take attendance and note the names of students not accounted for. (Staff should also note names of students who may not be on their roster.) Some school districts use colored cards to inform people supervising the school evacuation about unaccounted for students, e.g., after taking attendance and find-ing all students accounted for, a staff person would hold up a green card; after taking roll and finding some students missing, a staff person would hold up a red card; after taking roll and finding all students on the roster accounted for, but also finding other students who have "joined" the class during the evacua-tion, a staff person would hold up both green and red cards, thus notifying a person or people supervising the evacuation that all of the students are accounted for plus they have extra students in their group. The use of a colored card system may be very helpful during an evacuation and a chaotic scene.

- Students and staff should journey to the school's designated alternate site during at least one school evacuation drill each school year.

- Schools should consider practicing reverse evacuations—rapidly moving students/staff into a school building versus rapidly mov-ing students/staff out of the building.

- A media coverage site should not be near the school's evacuation site.

- In the event of a school evacuation to an alternate school site and the eventual dismissal of school, schools should consider moving students from the alternate site to a relocation site to unite students with their parents/guardians. Parents coming to the alternate site to pickup their students may cause confusion and, in some instances, overwhelm the alternate site. Parents should be instructed to pickup their students at a relocation site, thus enabling the school officials to provide an orderly and organized reunification of students and families. (In the event of a violence event impacting the school requiring an evacuation of students/staff and the presence of law enforcement in resolving the violent event, law enforcement personnel may need to interview stu-dents as to their knowledge of the event. Such interviews may occur at the alternate site. A parent presence at the site may hinder the interviews and cause unnecessary confusion. Releasing students who have been interviewed and moving them to a parent relocation site may provide a less confusing option. Parents should be informed of the school's designed pickup site at the beginning of each school year.

- Student medications stored in the health office or administrative office should be carried out of the school building during an evacuation. Student medications should be stored in a locked and secure area of the school. During a school evacuation drill, or during an actual building evacuation, medications necessary for student health should be taken from the school to the alternate site where students may be housed during the emergency.

- During a school evacuation, any materials necessary to maintain an orderly setting at an alternative school site should be taken from the school. Schools can use "To Go" kits for this purpose. A "To Go" kit can be anything from a box to a suitcase on wheels. Schools should have a minimum of two "To Go" kits. One kit should be stored in the administrative area and at least one other housed near an exit—usually a classroom or office. A person in the office should be responsible for taking one kit out of the school during evacuation drill or real event. A staff person should be assigned to take the backup kit out of the building during drills or actual events. Some important items for a school's "To Go" kit might be:

  * Student attendance lists.
  * Emergency phone numbers to contact parents.
  * A bull-horn—electronic speaker.
  * A roll of quarters. (There may be a need to use pay phones.)
  * A copy of the school's emergency plan.
  * First-aid items.
  * Keys to the alternate school site.
  * A map of the alternate school site.

Appendix A
Sample Crisis Response Manual

Overview

The purpose of this manual is to provide building administrators a quick reference guide to use in a crisis. It is the school philosophy that a planned and organized approach is more effective in reducing psychological and social difficulties following a crisis in school.

This Crisis Response Manual includes procedures designed to deal with a number of crises that could occur in the district. These procedures do not cover every condition that might develop and it may not always be possible to follow every step. This manual can be used in conjunction with your building emergency plans.

Utilizing the Crisis Response Team

The Crisis Response Team is a supportive service which can help schools assess, plan, and intervene in crises affecting staff and students. A planned, organized approach has been shown to be effective in reducing the emotional and social impact of a crisis. The Schools Crisis Response Team has specialized training to assist building administrators in directing crisis resolution activities.

To contact the Crisis Response Team call (24-Hour Crisis Line or name of team leader/administrator).

Crisis Response Team Services

- Meet with building administrators and key staff to formulate an action plan.
- Facilitate staff meetings to provide information related to the crisis.
- Support school staff.
- Help teachers process information with students.
- Work with students individually or in groups.
- Be available for contact with parents.
- Provide helpful, factual information to parents.
- Assist in handling media coverage.

Media Procedures

The only means to inform the general public is by the mass media; therefore, it is important to ensure the media receive prompt, accurate information. Isolated quotes from individuals can be incomplete or misleading and should be avoided.

After calling appropriate emergency personnel and following safety procedures:

- Notify the superintendent's office.
- Refer media contacts to the superintendent's office.
- Inform the office staff of the situation and how to handle phone inquiries.
- Recommend students and staff not talk to the media.
- Do not allow media personnel in the building.

Tips for Interviews

In the event it is determined to be appropriate and/or necessary for you to speak with the media:

- Be honest. If you don't know the answer to a question, say so. If you make a mistake in an interview, say so.
- There is no such thing as "off the record."
- If you are in a room with a microphone or a camera, always assume they are turned on.
- Try to have a goal for the interview. What do you want to accomplish?
- Prepare for the interview. If you need more time, ask for it.
- Understand what you are going to say so you can talk about the topic knowledgeably.
- Anticipate the "worst question" you may have to answer and plan for that in advance.
- Bridge a question from where you are in the interview to where you want to be.
- Never say "no comment." It makes it sound like you have something to hide.
- Don't use jargon. You won't have a translator.

Student/Staff Death

Immediate actions to be taken by building administrator(s).

Obtain facts concerning the death(s).

Notify the superintendent.

Notify the crisis team.

Decide on a time/place for a staff meeting.

Activate the building calling tree.

Follow through actions to be taken by building administrator(s) in conjunction with the crisis team.

Update information concerning the death(s).

Develop a plan for the day.

Meet with all building staff.

Make announcement to students.

Plan for subs if needed.

Notify other schools affected.

Identify students/staff most affected.

Administrator's Checklist for a Death in a Student's Immediate Family

Suggestions:

1. Verification of death (spouse, parent, hospital, police, sheriff, mortuary.)*

2. Inform the child's teacher(s).

3. Plan how to inform the child's peers (classmates).*

4. A visit to the family by appropriate school personnel (teacher, counselor, principal).

5. Arrange for a remembrance from the school (food, card, flowers).

6. Arrange for appropriate staff to attend services.

7. Identify people available to help the teacher talk with the student's classmates about the death and how to welcome a student back.

8. Assess counseling needs for the child when he or she returns to school (counselor/school social workers/school psychologist.

9. Plan and provide follow-up visit(s) with the family.

10. Provide student/family with information about community resources, if needed.

* Coordinate with other principals/buildings that may be involved.

Potential Suicide Checklist

Suicide threats must always be taken seriously and intervention should be immediate. If a situation is potentially life-threatening, students and staff need to recognize the issue of confidentiality does not apply.

What to do

Do not leave the individual alone.

Refer the individual to appropriate staff (administrator, counselor, school social worker) who will do the following:

Assess the degree of risk

Ask student directly if he or she is thinking of suicide.

If there is a plan, how specific is it?

How lethal is the method?

How available is the means?

Has there been a previous attempt?

Ask about feelings of anger and depression (crying, sleeplessness, loss of appetite, hopelessness).

Ask about losses (deaths, family changes, peer relationships).

Ask about any history of chemical use.

Ask whether the student has made final arrangements (giving away possessions, saying good-bye).

Intervention Plan

Contact student's parent(s) or guardian(s) and plan with them how to help the student.

Police and/or Child Protective Services may need to be involved if the parents are unable or unwilling to help.

Refer parent(s) or guardian(s) to appropriate services from physicians, mental health professionals and/or community agencies.

Police involvement may be required in situations where the student is assessed to be in immediate danger and the parents cannot be located or are unable to help. (School personnel should avoid transporting students in private vehicles.)

Follow-up

Complete the "Report of Suicide Risk" form and send to a designated administrator.

Check to be sure that the student has received (is receiving) appropriate services.

Plan for the student's transition back to school.

The student should have ongoing contact with a counselor/case manager.

Brief appropriate staff on the student's status.

Report of Suicide Risk

School	Date
Student Name	D.O.B.
Address	Parent Notified: Yes No
Parent's Name	Date of Notification
Telephone Number	Time
Staff Members Involved	Report Prepared By
Presenting Problem	
Recommendations	
Results of Parental Contact	
Action Taken	
Follow Up Will Be Done By	

Bus Accident

Principal and/or other school personnel need to go to the scene of the accident to identify and comfort students.

Someone needs to be available in the school office to answer questions.

The school should be ready to deal with the media.

Notify the crisis team, if appropriate.

Activate the calling tree, if appropriate.

Intruder in the Building

The first person to notice the intruder (person with a weapon or person who is upset or acting out of control) will notify the principal.

- The principal or a representative will sound a planned alarm, for example:
    1. In buildings with intercom system, "Mr. Green is in the building."
    2. Other buildings could use a long bell ring (10 seconds).
- Alarm sounded means: lock the classroom door, do not allow students to leave the classroom, be seated on the floor next to an interior wall away from windows and doors until further notice.
- Teachers take an accurate count of students.
- Designate personnel to monitor hallways and other areas of the building and to direct students not in class to a safe area.
- Staff communicates to office any information regarding the intruder.
- The principal will determine need to notify police and school superintendent of any emergency situation.

Hostage Situation

- Call 911.
- Avoid confrontations with the intruder before the police arrive.
- Principal or a representative will sound a pre-planned alarm, for example:
    1. In buildings with an intercom system, "Mrs. White is in the building."
    2. Other buildings could use a designated bell ring.
- Teachers should not allow students to leave the classroom and should direct them to be seated on the floor next to an interior wall away from windows and doors. Students should only be allowed to leave the classroom when the all-clear announcement is given or when directed to move to another location by the police, or a school administrator.
- Teachers take an accurate count of students.
- Designate personnel to monitor hallways and other areas of the building and to direct students not in class to a safe area.
- Notify the superintendent's office.
- Assign a staff member to liaison with police.
- Inform the office staff as to the appropriate information to give to callers.
- Make a list of those being held hostage.
- Refer media contacts to the superintendent's office.
- Plan how to inform the families of students and staff directly affected.
- Contact the crisis team to assist students and staff in dealing with the aftermath.

Mail Tampering (Anthrax, etc.)

Suspicious Package/Letter (Not Yet Opened)

1. Contact administrator.
2. Shut down heat/air handling equipment and all fans.
3. Isolate the room.

Contact Public Safety Officials

1. Triple bag the item in a sealable bag.
2. Treat isolated room as a crime scene.
3. Track package/letter. (Who handled the item.)

Administrator's Responsibility

1. Assist Public Safety personnel in keeping staff/students clear of isolated area.
2. Assist Public Safety personnel in determining who has handled the letter/package.

Suspicious Package Package/Letter (Opened)

1. Contact administrator.
2. Shut down heat/air handling equipment and all fans.
3. Isolate room.
4. Anyone who handled/opened the package will need to wash hands and arms as soon as possible with a mild soap and warm water. Anyone that has had direct contact with the substance will need to shower using warm water and a mild soap. They will need a change of clothes. The clothes warn should be triple bagged in sealable bags and may be used as evidence.

Contact Public Safety Officials

Administrators Duty

1. Assist Public Safety Officials in keeping area clear.
2. Assist in identifying who handled the package/letter.

Bomb Threat Procedures

1. Upon the receipt of a bomb threat, the person receiving the call will make every attempt to:
   a. Prolong the conversation. *Do not hang up the phone.* (Use another phone to call authorities.)

b. Identify background noises and any distinguishing voice characteristics.

c. Ask the caller for a description of the bomb, where it is, and when it is due to explode.

2. The person receiving the threat will notify the principal.

3. Call 911.

4. The principal will, in consulting with 911, decide whether to make a preliminary search or to evacuate the building.

5. The principal will notify the superintendent's office.

6. Inform staff and students of the bomb threat and any immediate directions, for example, remain in their rooms until an all-clear is given or directions to evacuate.

7. Ask staff to make a visual observation of their classrooms/work areas and inform them not to open cabinets, doors, or move objects. If anything suspicious is found, ***Do not touch it!*** The bomb can be almost anything from a bundle of dynamite to concealed or ordinary objects (briefcase, toolbox, or pieces of pipe). You will be searching for something that doesn't belong in the classroom/work area.

8. Check the absentee list and on each absentee from class at the time the threat was received. Account for all students, check halls and restrooms.

9. Ask for volunteers to participate in the search with the police/fire department.

10. Meet with the police/fire department and search team to decide on the procedure for checking the building.

11. If at any time the threat is determined to be valid, use standard fire drill procedures with any necessary modifications to evacuate the building. Evacuate at least 300 feet from the building. Plan for an alternate location if needed due to a prolonged search or inclement weather.

12. When the building is reported to be safe, resume whatever schedule is needed and debrief staff and students.

13. If a written threat is received, copy the contents and protect the original message (plastic or other covering) to preserve fingerprints and other identifying marks.

14. Use the Bomb Threat Checklist to gather helpful information.

Bomb Threat Checklist

Time _____ Date _____

Do not hang up. Use another phone to call police.
Record the exact words used by the caller

_____

_____

_____

_____

_____

Ask:
What time is the bomb set for? _____

Where is the bomb? _____

What does the bomb look like? _____

Why are you doing this? _____

Who are you? _____

Evaluate the voice of the caller:

Man _____   Accent _____

Woman _____   Speech impediment _____

Child _____   Intoxicated _____

Age (approx.) _____   Other _____

Background noise:

Music _____   Conversation _____

Children _____   Machine noise _____

Typing _____   Traffic _____

Airplanes _____   Other _____

Person receiving threat will immediately notify the principal.
Call received by _____

Sample Letter to Parents

To:

From:

Re: Emergency Procedures for Schools

The school district has developed a Crisis Response Plan that is designed to minimize danger to anyone occupying a school should an emergency occur. Our main objective is to attend to the health and welfare of your children in the event of a crisis.

In most emergencies your children will remain and be cared for at the school they attend. In the rare event of an emergency affecting the school your child attends that prohibits reentry to the building (such as a broken gas or water main, a fire or toxic spill), elementary students will be transported via school transportation to the nearest and most appropriate school building. Junior and senior high students will be dismissed to return home for the day.

We ask that you follow this procedure if you hear of any school emergency:

1. *Turn on your radio or television.* We will keep the media informed of any emergency.

2. *Please do not telephone the school.* We have limited phone lines. These MUST be used to respond to the emergency.

3. *Please do not come to the school unless requested to pick up your child.* Any emergency involving your child's school may mean emergency vehicles and workers must be able to get to the building. If the emergency necessitates relocation of staff and students, you will be informed via the media.

Please glue this information inside the cover of your phone book.

Chemical Spill/Toxic Fumes

If spill/fumes occur outside the school building:

Keep the students inside.

Close the windows.

Establish contact with police, fire, and health departments.

Establish contact with the superintendent's office.

Be prepared to evacuate the building.

If the students are outside, move upwind.

Don't step in spilled material.

Evacuation/Alternate School Locations

Although it is highly unlikely, some crisis situations may require the school be evacuated and the students be relocated. If emergency personnel determine the building will be unsafe for some time:

- Notify the superintendent's office.
- Make arrangements for the transportation of special needs students.
- Keep the media informed of evacuation/relocation plans so parents will have accurate information.

Elementary Schools

- Select and notify the nearest appropriate school building as an alternate site.
- Arrange for school transportation to relocate students.

Secondary Schools

- Junior and senior high students will be dismissed to return home for the day.

Calling Tree

- List the schools calling tree for contacting certified and classified staff.

Specific Building Plans

- Include plans specific to individual school buildings in the school district.

Appendix B
School Facilities Safety Assessment

Assessment Questions	Comments/Points to Consider
What security devices (classroom telephones, surveillance cameras, metal detectors, etc.) are in your school building(s)?	
Have unsafe areas of your school(s) been identified?	
What short-term and long-term plans have been developed to deal with unsafe areas?	
How many entrances are available for visitors to enter your schools?	
How many entrances for visitors are necessary?	
Which one(s) can be most easily monitored?	

School Facilities Safety Assessment

Assessment Questions	Comments/Points to Consider
What ways are available in your school(s) to communicate with staff during an emergency?	
Do you have an alternate site to take students and staff in the event of an evacuation of your school building(s).	
Have staff and/or students ever walked or been transported to the alternate site(s)?	
Do staff have keys to the alternate site(s)?	
What would happen with students if they needed to be at the alternate sites for 2 hours, 8 hours, or 24 hours?	

Dr. John Dudley

School Facilities Safety Assessment

Assessment Questions	Comments/Points to Consider
What is your school's criteria for identifying students who might be "at risk" regarding their own safety and/or the safety of other students or staff?	
Do you regularly assess your school climate (i.e. students, staff and parents attitude toward safety)? What do you use for school climate assessment and how to you share the assessment results?	
Are students given the opportunity to share their concerns about their personal safety at school? How? Where?	
Are staff members given the opportunity to share their personal safety concerns? How? Where?	
How are their concerns communicated?	

School Facilities Safety Assessment

Assessment Questions	Comments/Points to Consider
Do you have a district-wide common alert code for an intruder in a school building?	
Do all staff who work in the building including itinerate staff, know the code?	
Do all staff (certified/classified) have picture identification tags?	
Do you have multiple identification tags for staff (so they will wear them depending on choice of clothing)?	
Do you incorporate intruder, hostage or school shooting drills into your fire drills?	
Are staff required to take roll whenever your school building is doing an evacuation drill?	

School Facilities Safety Assessment

Assessment Questions	Comments/Points to Consider
Do you have student discipline procedures? Are they clearly written? Are they consistently enforced?	
Do you have a student sigh out procedure, which promotes student safety? Is it consistently followed?	
Do your school discipline procedures focus on the safety of non-offending students?	
How does your school monitor the progress of youth offenders returning to your school? How is this information shared about offenders?	
Are all staff who work with returning youth offenders involved in the monitoring process? If so, how? If not, why not?	

School Facilities Safety Assessment

Assessment Questions	Comments/Points to Consider
Does your school identify all students who could become at risk for dangerous behaviors? What criteria is used?	
If a student is potentially dangerous, are they removed from the general student body? What is the process for removal?	
Are alternative education programs available in your school(s)? Your community? Are they designed to help students with their personal issues as well as enhance their education?	

School Facilities Safety Assessment

Assessment Questions	Comments/Points to Consider
Does your school have a written plan to help manage a school crisis situation?	
Has the plan been written specifically for your school?	
Do all certified and classified staff have a copy of the plan?	
Have all staff been trained to use the plan?	
Is the plan reviewed annually? How?	
Is there a school crisis response team(s) in your school district?	

School Facilities Safety Assessment

Assessment Questions	Comments/Points to Consider
Has the crisis response team been trained to respond to a variety of school tragedies and crisis situations?	
What training have they received?	
Do they respond to school crises 24 hours a day, year round?	
Do you have a list of the crisis team leaders from other school districts in your area that have crisis teams?	
Which staff members are currently certified in firs aid/CPR training?	
How are they identified to staff and students?	

Dr. John Dudley

School Facilities Safety Assessment

Assessment Questions	Comments/Points to Consider
Does your school district have the same intruder code for all schools? If not, why?	
Are your school district's crisis plans current and relevant to each school building in your school district as well as your entire school district?	
Have school staff been trained in responding to bomb threats?	
Does staff know what to look for in their classrooms when there is a bomb threat?	
Have staff been trained in bomb evacuations and what to do in their classrooms before leaving them?	
Does your school district use curriculum or classroom lessons that focus on violence prevention?	

School Facilities Safety Assessment

Assessment Questions	Comments/Points to Consider
How do you communicate school safety concerns with your parents? The community at-large?	
How do you communicate your school discipline procedures with parents? The community at-large?	
How do you use local media to inform the community about school safety, student discipline, and alternative education programs?	
What parent education programs are available through your school district?	
How do you share common safety issues with law enforcement? Your community?	
How do you involve parents and community members in school staff development programs?	

Appendix C
General Guidelines for Responding to a School Violence Situation

- CALL FOR OUTSIDE AND/OR INTERNAL RESPONSE ASSISTANCE
  Pre-planning with law enforcement for school violence responses is important.

- INITIATE CODES (INTRUDER/HOSTAGE/BOMB) AS NECESSARY
  Codes should be the same for all buildings in the school district.

- DIRECT FIRST RESPONDERS
  Person meeting first responders should have keys to all building locations.
  Have an up-to-date map of the building available.

- IDENTIFY DECISION MAKERS
  Some schools have internal response teams, i.e. administrator(s), nurse, counselor, etc.

- CHECK STUDENT ATTENDANCE
  Red/Green cards (or your school colors) if building evacuated.

- SET UP COMMAND SITE(S)
  Have a regular command site. Have a backup command site.
  Backup command center should be away from the school office.
  Backup command center should have outside access.
  Backup command center should have communication capability.
  Identify command sites on school building map.

- CLEAR ACCESS TO ANY VICTIMS
  Unlock doors so first responders can enter the school.

- PREPARE FOR PARENT ARRIVAL
  Law enforcement may help with crowd control.
  Have parents report to a designated area or alternate school site.

- SET UP TRAFFIC CONTROL (IF NECESSARY)
  Pre-plan with law enforcement.

- IDENTIFY INJURED STUDENTS OR STAFF WHO HAVE BEEN TRANSPORTED
  Pre-plan communication links with area hospitals.

- INITIATE MEDIA PLANS
  See section III in School Violence-Prevention and Response guide
- PLAN FOR STAFF MEETING—INFORM STAFF
  Have crisis team(s) at the staff meeting.
  Do not allow media at or near the staff meeting.
- COOPERATE WITH LAW ENFORCEMENT
  Pre-planning with local and area law enforcement PRIOR to a school violence event is essential.
- PREPARE FOR THE IMPACT OF STRESS
  Use the school district's trained crisis team(s).
  Have backup substitute teachers available.
  Reconvene school at the earliest possible time.
  Identify students and staff in need of short and long term assistance.
  Don't underestimated the resilience of people.

School Violence and Response Preparedness Checklist

The following list of questions on school violence preparedness is general in nature. Add questions to the list the reflect unique needs in your school building or school district.

Question	Yes	No	Need to Consider
1. Does your school/school district have a comprehensive school crisis response plan?	❏	❏	❏
2. Is your school crisis response plan reviewed and/or updated annually?	❏	❏	❏
3. Does your school crisis plan address serious assaults on students or staff?	❏	❏	❏
4. Does your school crisis plan specify procedures if a bomb is found in the building?	❏	❏	❏
5. Does your school crisis plan address student and/or staff deaths outside of school?	❏	❏	❏
6. Does your school crisis plan address student and/or staff deaths occurring at school?	❏	❏	❏
7. Does your school have a trained school crisis response team(s)?	❏	❏	❏
8. Does your school crisis response team meet and practice on a regular basis?	❏	❏	❏
9. Does your school crisis response team have a floor plan of each building in the district?	❏	❏	❏
10. Do local and area law enforcement have an up-to-date floor plan of all buildings in the school district?	❏	❏	❏
11. Has your school district conducted meetings on responding to school violence with local and area law enforcement?	❏	❏	❏
12. Have you identified primary and secondary command sites in all school buildings?	❏	❏	❏
13. Do all identified command sites have direct access to the outside of the building and communications capability?	❏	❏	❏

Question	Yes	No	Need to Consider
14. Does your school district have a common word or phrase to alert staff of an emergency in the school?	❏	❏	❏
15. Do all staff have specific procedures to follow during a school emergency?	❏	❏	❏
16. Have all staff practiced procedures to be followed during a school emergency?	❏	❏	❏
17. Does your school have an alternate site in case of a school evacuation?	❏	❏	❏
18. Have staff and students practiced going to alternate sites?	❏	❏	❏
19. Do school staff have keys to access alternate sites?	❏	❏	❏
20. Are materials stored at the alternate sites to assist staff with student management?	❏	❏	❏
21. Is a copy of the school crisis plan stored at the alternate site?	❏	❏	❏
22. Does your school have an emergency kit, i.e., cell phone, master keys, list of all staff, hand-held radio, school crisis plan (in case of evacuation), first aid kit, etc.?	❏	❏	❏
23. Has staff been trained in intercepting or responding to intruders in the school?	❏	❏	❏
24. Have staff members trained in advanced first aid been identified?	❏	❏	❏
25. Is there a procedure for notifying advanced first aid trained staff to respond to an emergency in the school building?	❏	❏	❏

Dr. John Dudley

References

Aguilera, D.C. & Messick, J.M. (1992). *Crisis intervention: Therapy for psychological emergencies.* New York: Times Mirror.

Anderson, M., et.al. (2001). School-associated violent deaths in the United States, 1994-1999. *Journal of the American Medical Association, 286,* 2695-2702 (2001).

Borum, R. (2000). Assessing violence risk among youth. *Journal of Criminal Psychology, 56,* 1263-1288.

Boyd, J.H. & Moscicki, E.K. (1986). Firearms and youth suicide. *American Journal of Public Health, 76,*1240-1242.

Center for Disease Control. (1992). *Youth suicide prevention programs: A resource guide.* Public Health Service.

Cohn, J. (1987). *I had a friend named Peter: Talking to children about the death of a friend.* New York: William Morrow.

Davis, M. (1994). Critical incident stress debriefing: The case for corrections. *Corrections Forum.*

Fein, R.A., & Vossekuil, B.V. (1999). Assassination in the United States: A operational study of recent assassins, attackers, and near-lethal approaches. *Journal of Forensic Sciences, 44,* 321-333.

Flax, E. (1989). Aftermath: I would panic, but I would stick to my plan. *Education Week,* January 25, Volume 8, Issue 18, page 5.

Gibelman, M., et.al. (1991). *Resources in crisis intervention: School, family and community applications.* National Association of School Psychologists.

Graham, S. & Juvonen, JH. (2001) An attitutional approach to peer victimization. In Juvonen, J. Graham, S. (eds.), *Peer harassment in school: The plight of the vulnerable and victimized.* pp. 49-72. New York: Guilford Press.

Grollman, E. (1990). *Talking about death—A dialogue between parent and child.* Boston, MA: Beacon.

Holden, D. (1989). *Gran-Gran's best trick—A story for children who have lost someone they love.* New York: Magination.

Hannaford, M.J. & Popkin, M. (1992). *Windows: Healing and helping through loss.* Atlanta, GA.: Active Parenting.

James, J.W. & Cherry, F. (1988). *The grief recovery handbook: A step-by-step program for moving beyond loss.* New York: Harper & Row.

Jewett, C. (1982). *Helping children cope with separation and loss.* Harvard, MA: Harvard Common Press.

Joan, P. (1986). *Preventing teenage suicide.* New York: Human Sciences Press.

Kubler-Ross, E. (1981). *Living with death and dying.* New York: Macmillan.

LeShan, E. (1976). *Learning to say good-bye—When a parent dies.* New York: Maxmillian.

Manning, D. (1979). *Don't take my grief away.* New York: Harper Collins.

McKee, P.W., et.al. (1993). *Suicide and the school: A practical guide to suicide prevention.* Horsham, PA: LRP Publications.

Mellonie, B. & Ingpen, R. (1983). *Lifetimes: The beautiful way to explain death to children.* New York: Bantam Doubleday.

Nuland, S. (1994). *How we die: Reflections on life's final chapter.* New York: Alfred A. Knopf.

Pollack, W., & Shuster, T. (2000). *Real boys' voices.* New York: Random House.

Petersen, S. & Straub, R.L. (1992). *School crisis survival guide: Management techniques and materials for counselors and administrators.* West Nyack, NY: The Center for Applied Research In Education.

Ragouzeos, B. (1987). *The grieving student in the classroom.* Lancaster, PA: Hospice of Lancaster County.

Reddy, M. et.al. (2002). *Threat assessment in schools: A guide to managing threatening situations and creating safe school climates.* United States Secret Service.

Reddy, M. et.al. (2001). *Evaluating risk for targeted violence in schools: Comparing risk assessment, threat assessment, and other approaches.* Psychology in the Schools, 38, 157-172.

Sanford, D. (1986). *It must hurt a lot.* Portland, OR: Multnomah Press.

Stillman, P. (1979). *Answers to a child's questions about death.* Stamford, NY: Guideline Publications.

Tomerson, J. (2001, May). School violence: Sharing student information. Denver, CO: National Conference of State Legislatures.

U.S. Department of Education and U.S. Department of Justice (1999). 1999 Annual report on school safety. Washington DC: Authors.

Wolfelt, A. (1983). *Helping children cope with grief.* Muncie, IN: Accelerated Development.